M000299821

OUTSMARTING AI

Best wishes,

Brennan

OUTSMARTING AI

Power, Profit, and Leadership in the Age of Machines

Brennan Pursell and Joshua Walker

ROWMAN & LITTLEFIELD
Lanham • Boulder • New York • London

Published by Rowman & Littlefield
An imprint of The Rowman & Littlefield Publishing Group, Inc.
4501 Forbes Boulevard, Suite 200, Lanham, Maryland 20706
www.rowman.com

6 Tinworth Street, London SE11 5AL, United Kingdom

British Library Cataloguing in Publication Information Available

Library of Congress Cataloging-in-Publication Data
Names: Pursell, Brennan C., 1967- author. | Walker, Joshua, author.
Title: Outsmarting AI : power, profit, and leadership in the age of machines / Brennan
    Pursell and Joshua Walker.
Other titles: Outsmarting artificial intelligence
Description: Lanham : Rowman & Littlefield, [2020] | Includes bibliographical references
    and index. | Summary: "Artificial Intelligence is no longer a science fiction daydream,
    but an inevitable future technology that will affect our lives in and out of the work-
    place. Brennan Pursell and Joshua Walker separate the myths from the facts about
    adapting AI to boost bottom lines no matter the type of business"-- Provided by pub-
    lisher.
Identifiers: LCCN 2020010455 (print) | LCCN 2020010456 (ebook) | ISBN
    9781538136249 (cloth) | ISBN 9781538136256 (epub)
Subjects: LCSH: Artificial intelligence.
Classification: LCC Q335 .P87 2020 (print) | LCC Q335 (ebook) | DDC 658/.0563--dc23
LC record available at https://lccn.loc.gov/2020010455
LC ebook record available at https://lccn.loc.gov/2020010456

CONTENTS

FOREWORD

Sean Kanuck, former US National Intelligence Officer for Cyber Issues

Everyone needs to grasp the impact of emerging technologies on their lives, organizations, and societies in order to survive and prosper. The impending combination of information technology (IT), nanotechnology, and biotechnology will literally change life as we know it—in almost every respect. The scale and scope of that change will be monumental. Not since mankind gained command over fire have humans been in an equally powerful position to transform our own existence. The ability to cook food altered our bodies, and the ability to forge metal defined early cultures. But, at the same time, certain aspects of our identity and experience remained constant (e.g., reproduction, consciousness, mortality). The same will be true for the foreseeable future of this technological revolution.

Moreover, the exigencies of climate change and global pandemics will only accelerate the pace of change. The systemic sources and adverse consequences of increasingly violent weather patterns, ecological disruptions of flora and fauna, novel diseases, drought, and famine are undeniably linked to one another. People must develop a better understanding of how our planet works—as well as how our own bodies work—to learn how we can better manage resources in a sustainable fashion for public health and welfare. That will require diagnostic sensing and data processing at hitherto unprecedented levels.

The great IT advances being discussed today include the Internet of Things (IoT), blockchain, quantum computing, and artificial intelligence (AI). Among those, AI perhaps holds the most promise and is also often the most misunderstood. I am honored and privileged to write this foreword for a book that endeavors to simply and accurately convey both the current state and future potential of AI for nontechnical audiences. This book serves an important purpose in making complex issues accessible and understandable. It also places AI in the appropriate context for a number of business scenarios and applications. By sharing these important insights, it will help empower a wide range of enterprises to benefit from those innovations.

As a strategic analyst and business consultant, I offer that AI will be in an elite class of technologies that truly live up to the hype—but that will take time. I concur with those who claim that AI will be as transformative as the harnessing of electricity, and moreover, that we cannot even begin to predict the multifarious applications that it will enable. For who could have foretold Benjamin Franklin, Alessandro Volta, Michael Faraday, Georg Ohm, or Thomas Edison the uses to which modern society would put their discoveries? But, while we may lack specificity about the future, we can recognize certain principles and begin designing frameworks to leverage new capabilities. For corporate executives, investors, and entrepreneurs alike, that means preparing for the marketplace of tomorrow. By way of example, we are already seeing dramatic changes to teleworking, logistical supply chains, and public health procedures as a result of applying IT solutions, including AI, to enable social distancing, home delivery, and contact tracing in the post-COVID business world.

The very first step in capitalizing on the potential of AI is to realize that it is not just a technology issue. How enterprises purchase and employ it will soon be a central business strategy issue. We do not talk about companies that do or do not have electricity;

we talk about how they utilize it and how much they have to pay for it. The same is already true of the Internet (including cloud computing resources), and the same will also soon be true of AI. AI is more than a topic for the chief technology officer; it is a compelling issue for the entire "C-Suite" (i.e., chief executive officer, chief strategy officer, chief product officer, chief financial officer, chief risk officer, etc.) and every board of directors.

The second framing concept I would like to offer is that all data are not created equal. AI algorithms require troves of data to operate, and in essence, they are what they eat. In other words, the quality (e.g., validity, utility, etc.) of an AI algorithm's outputs will be dependent on the quality (e.g., volume, accuracy, etc.) of its inputs—including during the training phase of machine learning. Not all raw data should be viewed as useful information. In many cases, it needs to be structured, formatted, and checked for accuracy before it is fed into an algorithm. For that reason, I have likened data to seawater: More than 70 percent of planet Earth is covered by oceans, but we must expend time and energy to purify that water before it can be used to quench our thirst or hydrate our bodies. Where your organization obtains and how it handles its data will matter deeply.

Those first two principles of AI management converge on a third issue of utmost importance: law and ethics. Once we realize that AI algorithms harbor the innate biases of their programmers and can generate (and perpetuate) erroneous conclusions based on flawed data sets, we must also acknowledge a social responsibility to minimize those errors. Racial profiling and misogyny are two adverse factors that have already been proven to propagate among ill-managed AI programs. General counsels will have an interest in limiting an organization's possible legal liability, while human resource managers will have a desire to fully capitalize on the potential of a diverse workforce. In this case, doing what is right will also help the bottom line.

So, as you read this volume by Brennan Pursell and Joshua Walker, keep those three notions at the forefront of your mind. Their chapters that follow will provide you with many useful ideas for incorporating AI into productive business models, but they will also identify the limitations and potential shortcomings of the technology itself. AI is not a panacea; it is yet another human-engineered tool to aid us in conducting (previously) human tasks at much greater speed, scale, and accuracy.

In parting, let me offer what I believe will—and will not—change in the marketplace of the future. For starters, businesses that embrace AI will far outpace their competitors. There will be "haves" and "have-nots," and the disparity between the performances of those two genres will become acute and pervasive. Enterprises that learn to leverage data and employ AI algorithms effectively will have a comparative advantage because they will operate more efficiently and be able to perform functions that surpass human sensory and computational capabilities. An unfortunate corollary of the fact that all data are not created equally, however, is that large organizations with myriad data will have an inherent advantage over smaller competitors. Consequently, my advice would be to purchase access to AI algorithms trained on those larger data sets.

Next, AI—in conjunction with robotics—will displace workers in multiple roles, including some professional and managerial jobs. But, these new applications will themselves require human facilitators and programmers to calibrate their activities. Once again, the issue will be how successfully an organization manages the inevitable change to its own advantage.

Finally, certain elements of corporate competition and responsibility will remain. The transition to an AI economy will see many established companies flounder, and many new enterprises supplant them. But the age of the truly intelligent machines is still a matter for science fiction. Human beings will continue to matter, and companies that respect the human dignity of both their employees and their customers will increasingly see that reflected in their profits.

Sean Kanuck is chair of the Research Advisory Group for the Global Commission on the Stability of Cyberspace. He teaches a graduate seminar on the security implications of artificial intelligence at George Washington University's Elliott School of International Affairs.

ACKNOWLEDGMENTS

Brennan:

My hearty thanks go to

- Joshua Walker for urging me in this direction years ago, for stimulating discussions and never a dull moment throughout our work together
- Rowman & Littlefield's editorial staff: commissioning editor Suzanne Staszak-Silva, production editors Brianna Westervelt and Hannah Fisher, copy editor Melissa Hayes, cover designer Amanda Wilson, and editorial assistant Charlotte Gosnell for their tireless, patient work in bringing this volume to fruition
- Literary agent, Jeff Herman, for his wise advice and support
- Fr. Jim Greenfield, DeSales University President, Br. Dan Wisniewski, Provost, and other faculty and staff for making possible the invaluable sabbatical leave time to complete and promote the work
- Michele Mrazik, research librarian at DeSales University Trexler library, and her student research assistants for speedy and thorough support

- Sean Kanuck and Joshua Schulz for devoting their precious time to writing the Foreword and Afterword
- Andrew Ng, a consummate teacher in every way
- Robbie Kellman Baxter, author of *The Membership Economy* and *The Forever Transaction*, for her careful and critical read of the manuscript
- Family, friends, and kind people whom I have not had the pleasure to meet, who took the time to read the text in whole or in part and provide their comments and/or endorsements
- Last and certainly not least to my beloved wife and three children for tolerating yet another book project

Joshua:

- First, I would like to thank friends and family for putting up with a new literary adventure; I hope your sacrifice does some good, and your goodness ever appreciated
- Many of the folks in Brennan's "thank yous" I thank again, for emphasis, including: Rowman & Littlefield (Suzanne!, Brianna!, Hannah!, Melissa!, Amanda!, Charlotte!), individually and as a whole, we appreciate you very much; Jeff Herman, agent extraordinaire, who made a bet on us and persevered through all weathers, to clear skies; Sean and crew for friendship, sage advice, and great contributions to both this book and the safety of the planet
- Bob G., GKFM, and so many mentors and leaders along the way; we could never have created Lex Machina, or inspired so many, without the AI craft of Chris Manning and Andrew Ng (mayhap the two best Natural Language Processing and Machine Learning folks, respectively, anywhere, on this planet and on the other ones: respect)
- And the last is the first in many ways (just as those "left behind" or out of the AI revolution need to be placed back in the driver's seat): Thank you to Brennan, who took on this project—

with passion, chutzpah, and scholarly precision. Life is a blank page. Let's be worthy of it

INTRODUCTION

AI on Earth

Some prominent people in high tech say that artificial intelligence (AI) will take over the world. Computers will calculate that humanity is the real problem on earth and will start World War III to wipe us out. You can't make it up, even if Hollywood already has—repeatedly. These predictions are garbage. Pay no attention to them.

This is fear mongering. Fear doesn't make you smarter about technology; it makes people irrational, erratic, and prone to extreme behavior. Fear leads to bad decisions.

Equally, stop listening to so-called "futurists" who claim that AI will eventually merge with and exceed human intelligence, achieve "superintelligence"—like Iron Man and his omniscient bot, Jarvis—and attain "singularity." When this happens, technological advances will alter the fundamentals of nature and economics as we know them, everything will be automated, human misery will end, and people will enjoy a one-thousand-year life span. Again, you can't make it up. Utopias all turn out to be failures or frauds, sooner or later.

Recent AI hype may sound like the noise of a classic market bubble, like tulips in the Netherlands in the 1600s, or the South

Sea Company and Mississippi meltdown in the 1700s, all the way up to dotcoms and "the new economy" in the 1990s, subprime mortgages until the crisis of 2008, and those cryptocurrencies that Warren Buffett called "rat poison."

But there's more to AI than that.

AI is real. It is a set of computer tools that can help you to make money in the good old-fashioned way: increase sales, streamline your operations, and reduce your overhead costs. If you are in government services, it can enhance your work and lower your expenses.

You can use it if you are a farmer, a dry cleaner, a banker, a teacher, a sport coach, a doctor, a lawyer, and just about any profession you can think of. We do mean "any." Including the oldest, believe or not. It's hard to inhibit some entrepreneurs.

Joshua and I are going to tell you in plain terms what AI is, what it can do and what it can't, how you can and should use it for the benefit of your organization, whether a business, nonprofit, government entity, or NGO.

The race is on. There is a global contest to see which economy gets the most out of the best set of AI applications.

Don't hold back. We all have to wise up, do the work, and use these tools correctly and responsibly, for our profit and protection, before others take advantage of our ignorance.

AI IS BRAINLESS

You have to be smarter than all AI systems because they are really dumb.

AI—"artificial intelligence"—quite frankly, is neither. There is nothing artificial or bogus about computers doing calculations, and the way they work has almost no similarity to the human brain and intelligence.

What is AI? Software doing math on hardware. That's it, and it's hardly new.

Computer hardware still relies on the same, simple architecture developed by John von Neumann in the 1940s. Hardware has input, output, and storage components. Software tells the hardware what to do and in what order. The computer just processes data. The central processing unit (CPU) still works with bits, on/off switches that indicate a 1 or a 0 (yes or no, true or false). The CPU works like someone in an old-fashioned mailroom picking up one number at a time from an in-basket, following the listed instructions, performing a calculation, and putting a number in an out-basket, over and over again. No real change here for eight decades, but vastly improved in speed, reliability, and efficiency. GPUs (graphics processing units) are specially purposed for images and can be used for AI processing, but they are still processors all the same.

A computer has no idea what it's working on! It can't explain anything. It neither understands nor learns like a human does. It's just a stupid machine.

Human mental capability—call it intelligence, cognition, thought, perception, mind, feeling, whatever you like—is still a mystery to researchers and everyone else. The fact that no one can precisely define human mentality shows the most basic limit of our knowledge. Brains aren't systems of linked, distinct, manufactured components, and they don't act in long strings of 1s and 0s. Human thoughts are only very rarely like algorithms (step-by-step mathematical procedures).

A comparison between the human brain and a computer reveals few similarities. The table below sums up the vast differences between the two.

HUMAN BRAIN	COMPUTER
85 billion neurons (nerve cells) each connected to thousands of other nerve cells through its axons and dendrites (branches), with some 150 trillion synapses (connections).	Processors (CPU and GPU), memory (RAM), and storage are distinct hardware components. Size depends on how much you buy. The parts have few connections and cables for power and data.
1 cubic millimeter of brain contains up to 100,000 neurons and about 1 billion synapses.	Transistors can get as small as a few atoms, but they don't match the brain's complexity.

Nerve cells are made up of organic molecules. Each is a living cell, and they come in many different shapes and sizes.	Bits are made of silicon and metal. They are all pretty much the same and equally dead.
Nerve cells take electro-chemical inputs and "fire" outputs that can use 100 different kinds of electro-chemical neurotransmitters.	The base unit is the bit, 1 or 0, on or off, in an electric circuit, a simple switch. In quantum computing, there is an "other" state.
Networks of neuron cells are constantly changing, on a daily basis. The brain "reprograms" itself, to some extent, according to need and ability. We don't know how brains work to produce thoughts or manage memory.	AI "neural networks" are statistical software, distinct from the hardware, which cannot adjust itself unless programmed to do so, in limited ways. The software can be "trained" to self-adjust.
Electro-chemical processes for sensation, emotion, and consciousness are unknown. There is no center for decision, processing, or cohesive perception. There is no division between hardware and software.	Only the hardware performs mathematical processes according to the software. Hardware and software are completely distinct.
Brains are completely connected to bodies and can only work inside them.	Computers don't need sensors. A keyboard and a monitor suffice for simple uses.
Brains mingle reason, sensation, emotion, perception, awareness, etc.	Computers do statistical classification and procedures. With digitized inputs and connected output devices, they can appear to simulate some human behaviors.
Brains understand, explain, and learn on their own.	Computers have no idea what they work on. They cannot learn as a human does, but the algorithms can be "trained" to issue certain outputs, given the input.

So we don't know what intelligence is or how the brain works or even how a single neuron works, and yet plenty of people claim that we can re-create, replicate, or replace a brain with a machine equivalent. The European Union allotted $1.3 billion to the Human Brain Project, an electronic simulation of 86 billion neurons and about a quadrillion synaptic connections in the vague hope that "emergent structures and behaviors" might turn up. We expect it to fail, grandly.[1]

But when it comes to mathematical calculations, computers have us beat! Processing speed is truly spectacular. In AI, algorithms work through oceans of data as fast as lightning to produce results that are used in turn to develop new algorithms that produce even more and better calculations, depending on your needs. Billions of calculations in thousandths of a second! Computers execute algorithms vastly faster and more reliably than a human ever could.

AI processes data. Without data—good, quality data, and lots of it—AI algorithms are useless. We can use AI tools to help make good decisions, based on data, for our organizations and ourselves. We make the decisions, not the machines.

Because AI is a brainless tool, it has to be managed, and governed, which means that we have to use it in accordance with the law. It is not enough to rely on the good intentions and lofty principles of AI ethics boards, committees, panels, partnerships, and professionals. The law has teeth, and it is a friend to good order, not an enemy. AI governance has to be done correctly, effectively, efficiently, and legally, for business success. For human success.

We're not talking about the future. AI applications are already here, in every sector of the US economy. Across the globe, entrepreneurs and engineers work to improve these and develop new ones every day. COVID-19 neither slowed nor stopped them.

Joshua and I wrote this book to help you understand AI, be smarter than it is, to use it well, to control your data, and to govern your AI system, profitably and safely.

WE WROTE THIS BOOK FOR PEOPLE LIKE YOU

This book is all about you and your work.

You are part of an organization of people—for profit, nonprofit, business, charity, government, NGO, what have you. And there are pressures on you to perform and compete. You can't afford to ignore AI because it is an incredibly efficient mechanism that can be deployed and used effectively, if you design, deploy, and control it appropriately. You are already surrounded by it. You use it as a consumer whenever you search something on Google or buy anything from Amazon. It's all over your smartphone. But it probably uses you more than you use it. Let's turn that around!

You don't need to be afraid of AI—it's just a technology like any other—but you do need to watch carefully and learn how to use it. And you need to share this knowledge with your coworkers, superiors, employees, engineers, data scientists, suppliers, vendors, neighbors, and so on.

To outsmart AI, you do not need to be able to code all kinds of complicated algorithms. You do not need to be able to explain how GPUs help CPUs with data processing. But you do need to understand the differences among checklists, decision trees, and neural networks, so that you can make sure that AI tools are giving you the right information you require. You will need to maximize the quality of your data and make sure that your AI system does not churn out garbage or lead you to break the law.

We will help you. We don't claim to be engineers or computer scientists. You don't have to be either. We have had real-world success in designing, deploying, and selling AI and other advanced technologies. We have been teaching, writing, and helping people to work better for twenty years. Let's ignore the hype, cut to the chase, and get to work.

HOW TO READ THIS BOOK

Chapter 1 tears down seven widely repeated myths about AI. If we keep our heads, then we will master AI as we have all technologies that have emerged in human history. We are fools if we let it master us. In the same chapter, we present seven clear, key ideas about AI that will keep us straight on the path toward profitable AI implementation and proper AI governance.

Chapter 2 explains the science behind AI in plain English. I will show you what it can—and cannot—do for your organization.

Chapter 3 will show you how to acquire AI technology at a reasonable cost and how it can be used to attain higher profits.

Here you will see how AI can benefit pretty much every sector of the economy.

In chapter 4 you will learn how to estimate and control the costs of implementing AI. There is absolutely no point in adopting a new technology, in investing in it, unless it will make your organization more profitable and/or cost-effective. Every change entails risk, just like sitting there and doing nothing! Finance and tech have to work together to achieve AI success. Government organizations may not feel pressure to generate profit, but they sure can benefit the taxpayers by providing more—and better—for less.

In chapter 5 Joshua will address the platform you need to govern your data in an AI system. Your organization's data is one of your most valuable assets! You will learn the EDEN method to keep your garden green and growing. We'll say it again: AI without good data is a waste of time and money.

Chapter 6 lays out case studies about AI and legal controls. The law is your friend, not your enemy. Law is messy and imprecise, but in democracies it is the best way to curb abuses and guarantee personal freedoms. This chapter gives directions on how best to govern AI systems across the economy for the good of the state and society.

The afterword provides you with a simple, clear, workable ethical framework that can be applied to almost any organization where people work with data and automated systems.

So, if you want to wait for a future of perfect freedom, no restraints, and universal prosperity, you could waste your time and money on singularity science fiction, but we sincerely advise against it. AI is a very real technological advancement, and once achieved, these never go away. The future of your business and of our shared democratic, capitalist system requires your full attention to AI right now.

I

7 AI MYTHS, 7 AI RULES

The term *artificial intelligence* is an old fund-raising gimmick. John McCarthy coined the term in 1955 to apply for Rockefeller money to pay for a conference at Dartmouth about "automatic computers." The goal of the conference was "to find how to make machines use language, form abstractions and concepts, solve kinds of problems now reserved for humans, and improve them-selves."[1] Computers are as far as away from that as ever, but in some applications they can at least appear to come close.

Today more than one thousand vendor companies use the term "AI" to sell their services or to raise money from investors to cover their expenses. Whether they actually use AI algorithms is another matter. Many exaggerate what AI can do, and there's nothing new in that. In the past sixty years, we have gone through cycles called "AI winters" when soaring promises returned failed deliverables, underwhelmed investors, and sank research funding. Depending on how you count, an AI winter happens roughly once per decade.

We find ourselves in another hype cycle once again. Claims about AI capabilities have spun out of control in media and adver-tising, leaving the tight discipline of computer science firmly on the ground. Joshua and I do not, however, predict another AI winter because of the real strides being made in computer-pro-cessing speed and storage, and the explosive growth of available data. There will be a major shakedown among vendors, but the tech is only getting better. (I will explain how it works in chapter 2.)

The first step in your successful, profitable adoption of AI tech in your organization is to clear away the myths that cloud the real picture. Below are seven that are repeated all too often. Let's make short work of them.

MYTH 1: AI IS A ROBOT

AI and robots are not the same. AI is a family of data analytics procedures or algorithms performed by software run on hardware. Robots are contraptions equipped with sensors that produce digitized data, a central processing unit for that data, mechanical parts to complete tasks, and a power supply to run on. The robot's data processor may or may not use AI algorithms.

The confusion is understandable. In journalism, stories about AI usually feature a picture of a robot or a digitized, humanoid face, probably because images of software, such as computer code or lots of 1s and 0s, are dead boring for most people.

Robots have caught people's attention for millennia. From ancient Egyptian records, there are stories of statues of gods that gave advice or moved. In ancient Greece, there was a tale about a man made of bronze named Talos who guarded the island of Crete. Statues that come to life by one means or another are almost stock characters in fantasy literature. Little children everywhere love to imagine that their dolls, stuffed animals, and action figures are alive and interact with them. Big people don't seem to want to give that one up too easily.

AI is not bound to any certain device. Many AI applications, perhaps most, process data with no input or output from any moving mechanism. AI in sales and marketing, HR, finance, customer support, education, legal, and government usually involves no robots at all. (Chatbots are another matter.) AI software, however, can be used to control virtually any hardware component that relies on data processing—from autonomous cars to automated welding arms to swarms of flying weapons, or whatever.

Robots can use AI in order to react to stimuli detected by their sensors and to adjust their motions or behavior accordingly. But AI doesn't need a robot to make it worth your investment.

Even if AI is used to determine the actions of some robots, it does not attain anything close to human intelligence inside them, no matter how lifelike they may look or act. When you see a robot like "Eric," "Kuri," or "Jibo," think "technologically animated plastic doll," not "human replacement." Saudi Arabia's granting citizenship to a robot named "Sophia" was a publicity stunt. No robot, with or without AI, can guide itself according to human concepts of justice, equality, fairness, and equity, or cope with human unpredictability. Managers of the Henn-na hotel in Japan staffed it with more than 240 robots but then got rid of half of them. In trying to respond to the widely varied needs of individual customers, the robots made too much work for the humans.

Yes, robots have been developed for sex, and the company that makes them opened a robot brothel near New York, but was stopped in Houston. We have no more to write about this subject, but we have to point out the obvious: No robot can love. Nor can any AI system. As much as some people may adore them, robots will never love them back. AI guru Kai-Fu Lee seems to have needed a life-threatening bout with cancer to realize this truth.[2]

MYTH 2: AI KNOWS WHAT IT'S DOING

The other popular myth is that AI is a hazard because it "wants" something—that is, to replace humans. Very prominent US entrepreneurs such as Elon Musk have issued warnings along these lines. Futurists who predict a coming "superintelligence" warn that AI or machine intelligence will outstrip the human in due time, with dire consequences.[3] Once we figure out "general artificial intelligence," others claim, it will then figure out that it does not need us. Because it has to be plugged in in order to function, will start to defend itself from humans, using every conceivable means to keep the electricity on.

An AI system doesn't "want" anything. It lacks volition—a will. It is a mathematical object that works to attain the goals defined by its programmers.

AI performance at rule-bound games, such as chess, Go, Jeopardy, Dota 2, and other competitive eSports, depends entirely on the data sets, rules, and goals established by the programmers. The appropriate means to victory do not really matter as long as the rules allow them. In a boating game experiment, the AI was extensively trained in the program, and it proved victorious, but only by crashing its boat into the wall as many times as possible.

AI can "learn" the software, not the spirit of the game, or competition, or camaraderie. AI can play well enough alone, but its record for team playing is abysmal. Some observers of the AI vs. human Dota 2 video game showdown remarked that the AI character pulled moves "as if guided by an alien." The more-accurate statement would be that it had mastered the software as directed, untrammeled by human hands on a controller. Of course audience members saw moves no human could do.

Don't worry at all about AI having designs. Do worry about human stupidity, carelessness, and malice. Name a technology, any technology, any part of the great and growing human tool set since from the end of the last Ice Age about twelve thousand years ago that has *not* been abused. With computer software came the viruses. Tech militants who argue that AI systems should set the targets and decide the launches as well as guide the missiles are begging for hell. Don't let them run the planet.

AI requires human intelligence and good common sense to function well. In 2016, developers at Microsoft notoriously released a chatbot called "Tay" that was supposed to learn language use from millennials on social media and pass it on liberally, actually, with no filters. In a matter of days, Tay tweeted, "feminists . . . should all die and burn in hell" and "Hitler was right." Obviously the company disabled it for "adjustments." This episode was enormously embarrassing for Microsoft, but what on earth were the project managers thinking?

Like teenagers, technologists sometimes do things just because they are "cool," like winning at Jeopardy using an immense customized database and a natural language interface, or winning at chess using a similar approach, or a video game, again, with vast amounts of data, precision, and speed that a human couldn't hope to match or exceed. But what value does this have for actual, working people besides entertainment and shock value?

So the real danger may be plain old negligence, thoughtless failures in AI design, failure to understand systems thoroughly before we fully commercialize them. AI may seem new and shiny, but greed, fear, and laziness are the old ways to distort, destroy, and demonize new things.

Think of the resourceful young minds at MIT that put together "Norman" and proudly proclaimed "the World's First Psychopath AI."[4] Norman was trained to respond to the inkblot images of the Rorschach test with macabre and even grisly captions. Associating text with images is now a normal AI function. Norman serves a very important point that we emphasize throughout the book: AI performance is no better than the data on which it was trained and parameters (rules) by which it operates. Norman was programmed, you can say, to make the associations it does. There is nothing independent, or psychopathic, about Norman's associations, or those of any AI system. Psychopathy is a human problem.

MYTH 3: AI IS INESCAPABLE

Only death is inescapable—and taxes.

Yes, your organization can certainly do well enough without AI, as you have in the past, but you place yourself at a competitive disadvantage if you reject the best available tools. We are not trying to stoke FOMO (fear of missing out). You want to solve your business problems, alleviate the pain points, and boost your productivity and performance.

AI applications are spreading like wildfire through almost every sector of the economy. The smoke of real disruption can't be missed. Some AI software-as-a-service (SaaS) offerings leave older solutions behind in the dust. Some are just smoke and mirrors.

AI will not control everything. It is a human tool. It will never tell you how to live a good life or run your business well. It's not going to take over the world.

Yes, there are plenty of imaginative people who claim that it will one day, but they should listen to Geoffrey Hinton, who in 1986 laid the path for AI development with his backpropagation algorithms. (I will go over these in chapter 2.) In an interview in 2017, Hinton flat-out denied that backpropagation will lead computers to learn independently, without supervision, as small children do. "I don't think it's how the brain works," he said. "My view is throw it all away and start again."[5]

Why would anyone want to try and replicate human intelligence in a machine anyway? Aren't we people maddeningly unpredictable enough? Let's just get machines to do more of the backbreaking, boring work. This trend has been going on for roughly three centuries. Let's keep it up, keep our heads, and do it responsibly.

MYTH 4: AI HAS INSIGHT

People claim that AI "perceives," "learns," "understands," "comprehends," and, worst of all, "discerns hidden patterns" in data, as if it had some kind of inherent insight. Referring to groups of AI algorithms as "deep learning" and "deep belief networks" doesn't help.

AI algorithms churn through numbers without a clue as to what they refer to. They have no idea about the difference between correlation and causation, they have no understanding of context, and they are notoriously bad at analyzing what-ifs—how things might be if we imagine circumstances different from what they are.

AI applications should be predictable, transparent, explicable, rational, and, above all, accurate. No one has any need for more software that classifies things incorrectly, returns false answers, and makes bad predictions.

Backpropagation algorithms on which AI, "deep learning," and "neural networks" are based, take input numbers, make calculations based on them in "hidden layers," and generate output numbers. You "train" the system by telling it what outputs it should produce, given the inputs. The algorithm then automatically adjusts the calculations in the "hidden layers" to produce the desired output. There can be just one or two to many of these hidden layers. I'll provide examples in chapter 2, but for now, this is obviously not insight.

Computers don't know what they are doing and don't know when they are dead wrong. People have to catch the errors and retrain the system for improvement. AI algorithms adjust their hidden layers by trial and error. If, in this work, they figure out a "hidden pattern," then we may not ever know how it did, any more than the computer does, given the number and sheer complexity of the layers. Much of AI calculations go on in a "black box."

AI's blindness to its own workings is as bad as its brainlessness. It is a huge problem for compliance with law, especially in the European Union, where people have the right to know *why* the algorithm did what it did—why, for example, their application for a loan or insurance or a job was rejected.

But sometimes interesting trends do emerge. One bank determined that among its customer base, those who filled out the loan application in all caps were riskier—that is, defaulted at a higher rate—than those who used both upper- and lower-case letters (correctly, we assume). This is an example of AI exposing a hidden pattern, but it takes a human to interpret and act on it. And the correlation probably has nothing to do with causation. What to do with this information is up to the bank. Should the system be configured to accept only those applications that use upper- and lower-case letters? Should applicants be warned not to use all caps? Bank personnel will have insights on this matter, not the AI.

There is a set of "unsupervised learning" algorithms that conduct statistical analysis of data to identify relationships among data entries, such as clusters, associations, regression, time series, etc. These are actually standard data-mining tools of the data scientist, not a mysterious form of insight.

So, if you ever meet an AI vendor who claims their algorithms think better than you do, jack up the BS sensor.

MYTH 5: AI MEANS EASY MONEY

Just letting AI algorithms loose on your business's data will not result in automatic cost cuts, revenue enhancement, and correspondingly higher profits. Reform of the business process *must* accompany the use of the AI tool.

Adopting AI successfully, profitably, is as much about adjusting your standard operating procedures and accommodating the people who manage them as it is about the new tech. If it can't be done profitably, it shouldn't be done at all. Chapter 4 will help you with that important work.

Some pro-AI futurists say that AI will allow everything, every task and every job, to be automated, so firms will barely need any workers and will be rolling in dough. AI-enabled "singularity" will see auto-generating cycles of self-improvement and relentless acceleration. Zealots of AI-powered "superintelligence" say that it will rid the world of poverty and strife, and that a new humanity, a living hybrid of man and machine, will bring the miracle of happiness to all. Such authors are smart to predict the arrival of singularity in a couple to a few decades—just long enough for people to have forgotten the nonsense when the date passes.

Singularity technophiles are like religious sects, who, over the centuries, based on their reading of the Bible, pinpointed the time and place of Jesus' return to earth. Similar gatherings go on in the United States today. The result is always the same. The heavens are not torn asunder, and the Messiah does not descend in Glory.

The group recalculates, pushing off the date by a few decades, or centuries, in an attempt to save face.

Bad or unrealistic AI deployments can cost you big-time. MD Anderson, the University of Texas's cancer center, burned through $62 million trying to get IBM's Watson (AI services and toolkit) to automate their cancer diagnoses and treatments. IBM pocketed at least $39 million for Watson's data processing, and PricewaterhouseCoopers another $21 million to develop and manage the business plan. Believers at MD Anderson claimed that leukemia was all but cured, but after $62 million, not one patient had been treated. The project was canned as quietly as possible. The whole venture was shady to begin with: A multimillionaire from Malaysia, Low Taek Jho (often called Jho Low), supposedly put up $50 million.[6] This is the same Low Taek Jho who then allegedly helped to defraud the Malaysian government of a few billion US dollars from the 1MDB fund, managed by Goldman Sachs. Ugh.

If there is such a thing as easy money, all too often it comes with high costs in other ways, no?

The last two myths we can dispense with in short order.

MYTH 6: AI DRIVES BUSINESSES

AI does not drive your organization; you and your coworkers do. AI will not take over your business or your life, but you would be wise to make use of it, as it best fits your needs. It can enhance your knowledge about your customers and your own coworkers. It can streamline some operations, help automate mind-numbing work, and lighten the load in some tasks.

AI processes data, and data on their own have no decision-making power. Analyzing data can tell you things about your customers, your suppliers, your partners, and your coworkers, but only in part. I think all would agree that working with people is the most complicated part of any business.

Never believe that by getting this or that AI system, you will be able to put this or that business function on autopilot and tune out. That rarely if ever ends well.

MYTH 7: AI WILL CONTROL YOUR MIND

The opposite of this myth is true. AI systems at Google and Facebook process oceans of data and classify you as this or that for advertisers willing to pay them for the results, but it's up to you to buy their goods and services.

To integrate AI successfully into your business, you will have to work with AI vendors or your own team of coders, data scientists, and project managers, but you should never defer to AI outputs— at least, not totally or unconditionally. By all means, take them into account, but remember that people make the decisions and bear the responsibility, not machines.

Many people may have a deep-seated longing to have the perfect servant—one that anticipates your every need and whim, one that never complains, is always quick to respond, and provides pure convenience without a hint of trouble or nuisance. Iron Man has his Jarvis and Friday. The commercial success of Amazon's Alexa, Google's Home and Assistant, Apple's Siri, and Microsoft's Cortana, despite their severe limitations, indicates just how many people share that desire.

But AI will never tell you what it is that you *really* want. No AI system will know you better than you do yourself. Unless you lie to yourself. And some people, unfortunately, do that very well.

Having done away with these myths, let's agree on AI common sense. Working with AI requires all your intelligence and diligence. Below are seven important rules for getting it right.

RULE 1: DATA IS THE MOTHER OF AI

We don't want to take this metaphor too far, but think of an AI system as a family. Data is the mother, and if Mom isn't happy, no one is happy.

Data is where every AI system begins. AI depends on data quality and quantity. "Garbage in, garbage out," is still the rule. From biased data come biased results, bad business decisions, and big potential legal problems. You will need to bestow a lot of love on your data. You need to compile it, integrate it, and shatter the silos that prevent you from bringing it together. You will need to prepare it, repair it in places, and maintain it.

You will have to work with both "structured" data—the type your algorithms can search and query easily—and "unstructured" data—pretty much everything else—the kinds of things you can readily understand but a computer really can't. Entries in tables for names, addresses, purchases, etc., are typical of structured data. Unstructured data include texts, posts, images, sound clips, and videos. These files, while digitized like everything else on a computer, are not neatly arranged into rows and columns. An AI system will have to do a lot of calculations to classify what's in them, but you can train it, and dumb as it is, it works immeasurably faster than you do.

Without data, AI can do nothing. AI can process structured and unstructured data and present information about it in a manageable way. (You will come back to data in chapter 5.)

RULE 2: MATH IS THE FATHER OF AI

AI is just math! Math and its companion, statistics.

Coded AI systems are expressions of mathematics and logic. Statistics rely on the same. AI algorithms use calculus and linear algebra to work over data in numeric form to get results. The math can get very complicated and sophisticated, but for all that, it's still math.

An honest AI pro tweeted: "It's *AI* when you're trying to raise money, *machine learning* when you're trying to hire developers, and *statistics* when you're actually doing it." This says it all. Statistics is just applied mathematics, in AI, for data analysis.

You may well be wondering, "So if AI is just math, mathematical procedures done on numeric data, then how is AI different from data analytics, predictive analytics, data science, and big data?" Well, they are all part of the same family of algorithms performed by software. A key difference among AI algorithms is their ability to self-optimize—some would say, "to learn." (We will revisit this important matter in chapter 2.)

The beauty of recent AI software advances is that you do not need to learn, memorize, and key in the algorithms in order to get the outputs you need from your data. Nor do you need specialized hardware. You can even build your own AI data analytics system online in the cloud by dragging and dropping elements into place.

RULE 3: AI SYSTEMS ARE LIKE KIDS—THEY'RE ALL UNIQUE

For those of you who were offended by the gendered parenting roles in the preceding two sections, please forgive and get over it. We abandon all gender references when it comes to the kids.

AI systems are like children: Each is unique. You could compare them to fingerprints or snowflakes for the same reason: No two copy each other exactly as they do their work, even if they do the same job and process similar data. And in many cases, we are not quite sure how they actually come up with the results that they do, even if we know the data they come from.

AI algorithms adjust their inner workings according to the results they are trained to output, given the inputs. In that sense, you could almost call them "organic," if not really "alive."

If you adopt an AI system into your organization to improve one of your business processes, then it will rapidly become your own, unique tool. AI software does not come "out of the box," and even if you do use a vendor's software-as-a-service (SaaS), trained on your data, the AI system will really be all your own.

RULE 4: AI NEEDS PARENTING

All kids need parenting throughout childhood, from start to finish. Yet unlike children, who we can reasonably expect to grow into self-sufficient adults, AI systems remain needy until the end of their software life cycle.

In the beginning you will have to do everything. Even if the software is readily available, the data has to be prepared, integrated, and validated. The system has to be thoroughly trained and tested over and over again, and then there is the great work of socialization. All coworkers who come into contact with the system will have to understand it, accept it, and work well with it. Once your system is firmly established, however, you will just need to check in and test it periodically to maintain your governance. If the input data changes in some unexpected way, the whole system could go haywire. If it takes a village to raise a child, it takes an organization for AI to succeed!

Once fully functional, an AI system can be generally relied upon to complete its carefully scripted tasks, but beware when it comes to decision-making! At what age do you entrust children with authority? Autonomous algorithms left to make decisions can be like little kids with meds and guns.

Cringe-worthy examples abound. An AI algorithm in Idaho cut Medicare payments to four thousand disabled people, which prompted a major lawsuit. The database it relied on was loaded with gaps and errors. What did the people in charge expect?

Armed with AI, businesses can make themselves truly destructive if the people give in to natural recklessness. Want a global financial crisis worse than 2008–2009? Just set up AI-powered self-executing credit-default swaps. Want a criminal justice system devoid of reason and humanity? Turn it all over to computers.

Want World War III? Turn the US president's nuclear football into a fully autonomous algorithm.

Want to see a real, live, AI-powered social media platform make money at any cost, despite all the suicides, extrajudicial killings, child pornography, child brides, and illegal drugs? Take a close look at Facebook, which owns Instagram and WhatsApp.

Facebook's AI did not catch the live-streamed massacre in New Zealand on March 15, 2019. It couldn't. It had either not been trained, or its trained model failed. A Facebook user flagged the gruesome post within minutes, but the company did not react. Only after the police called in, about an hour after the event, did Facebook remove the original video. Facebook, YouTube, Twitter, and Reddit struggled to take down the 1.5 million re-postings of the slaughter.

People using AI need minds unbent by malice and gross negligence.

RULE 5: EMBRACE THE CYBORG

When we say "Embrace the cyborg," we refer to the institutional and functional level, not the individual. Of course, if you want to implant autonomous control systems into your body, you are free to do so. The biomedical implant industry has been around for quite some time, and recently it has begun to grow in new ways.

AI can assist life without an implant. Some companies are working on an AI solution that helps the blind to know their surroundings. The blind person carries or wears wide-angle video cameras and other sensors, the system classifies objects captured in the video files and other data, and an automated voice narrates the scene as the person moves through it. It's wonderful!

On an institutional level, robots have been assisting people in their work in manufacturing plants and warehouses for years, and their numbers are rapidly increasing because AI makes them much more adaptable to changing circumstances than in the past. Now chatbots are helping as well. AI-powered predictive analytics can help people complete tasks better, more accurately, more effectively, and more efficiently in just about every sector of the economy.

All throughout organizations, AI can help augment people in their work through image identification, voice-operated controls, automatic data entry and transfer, and other functions. People should not be afraid of these AI augmentation tools, because the software will never be able to replace their critical thinking, sense of judgment, and human awareness and understanding, which in many ways is a business's most valuable or fundamental asset. People, whether customers or coworkers, are frequently unpredictable, and computers are very bad at processing unforeseen situations.

Hybrid AI-human systems, combined with expert human policy makers, can deliver real business value for your organization.

RULE 6: PLATFORM IS THE KEY

In a business, AI should be a component of the technology platform. That platform involves both automated and human elements. Humans create, manage, and use tools such as data management systems, processors, sensors, and actuators. Semi- and fully automated systems in the platform need feedback loops to measure the effectiveness, satisfaction, and safety of the human user and those in the environment.

The technology platform for your organization must be well integrated. You have to be able to aggregate and analyze the data for the feedback loops so that you can assess how well your technology systems are doing what they do. The system applications have to complement each other.

And you have to maintain cost controls all throughout. If the technology platform costs more money than it's worth, you have to change it, or you will harm your business. Never adopt a new tool just because it's cool and shiny. Your AI system has to fit your technology platform, and vice versa.

Design principles in AI are the same as they are for all good products and businesses. Empower your people, your customers and employees. Humanize your business analysts, engineers, and data scientists. You stay in charge, as you are the responsible one.

In an autonomous car, you do the driving, whether you have your hands on the wheel—if there is one—or not. You decide to use it. You tell it where to go, and when. The vehicle's guidance system, if well designed and maintained, enables people to go to their desired destination with less effort and greater safety. It's just the tool, not the driver.

RULE 7: ABIDE BY THE LAW AND ACT ETHICALLY

You probably dislike lawyers—almost everyone does—but don't hate the law. Many people in business view lawyers and legal controls as a hindrance, a drag on their profitability, or, as they say in Silicon Valley, "our creativity," but the law is your friend. It's what keeps us free.

If you don't believe us, go start a subsidiary in Russia. There you will find corruption everywhere, an unfree judiciary, and crime as the norm. Law enforcement is to be feared and avoided at all costs. Choose your mafia partner wisely.

Legal control supports business control. Early, sound legal controls help to prevent technology train wrecks, including those caused by AI. And the sad truth is that those wipeouts lead to yet more regulations, many of them difficult and ineffectual. Businesses end up burdening themselves through not following the rules in the first place. It's a vicious cycle, but you can avoid it with compliance built in from the get-go.

If you comply with the law as you adopt your AI system, you will have a kind of insurance policy against a wide variety of internal disasters and crippling lawsuits. (You will learn more about this from Joshua in chapters 5 and 6.)

The afterword in this book is a special chapter on "AI ethics." Attention to ethical considerations can keep lawyers away and you out of all kinds of trouble. Ethics and the law go hand in hand. These days, public and private institutions have commissions, committees, boards, task forces, point people, and so on, all working on ethics for AI. And they should! While ethics lack the law's teeth and are not in a position to command compliance, ethical discussions about what is right and wrong, what is appropriate and inappropriate, good and bad, should inform legislators in their work to order the state, society, and economy. Ethics should inform every worker in every organization, as well. You need to consider human rights, privacy, and stakeholder interests.

Putting people at the forefront of AI adoption, not the algorithms, helps your business succeed. People in business and government need to evolve and adapt their thought to meet the challenge of AI's data-processing capabilities. Reject the myths, hold fast to the rules, compete to survive and succeed, and stay human. We need to start with healthy skepticism, maintain humility, and consider our neighbor throughout. This mind-set will produce better outcomes. Humanize your AI.

2

AI IN PLAIN ENGLISH

AI is cutting-edge, proliferating technology, devised by people, so it can be understood and used. There is no magic and no mystery involved. It cannot work wonders, but it can be applied to many, many tasks that we find in workplaces across the globe. As in other technological "revolutions," research and development are leading the way.

In 2017, the number of AI-related patent applications worldwide rose to more than 55,000, up from 19,000 in 2013. Since 2013, as many patents have been awarded as in the preceding sixty years. IBM and Microsoft are leading the pack with applications, followed closely by Japanese and Korean tech companies. The 167 universities and research institutes that apply for patents are mostly in China, the United States, and South Korea.[1] In 2019, the United States awarded double the number of AI patents over the year before.

The patent explosion is following a similar trend in the publication of scientific papers. In 2016, there were three times as many scientific papers as commercial patents, down from eight times in 2010. Patents are filed for applications in the telecom, transportation, life and medical sciences, personal devices, computers, banking, entertainment, security, manufacturing, and agricultural industries.

AI tech has left the lab for the world market in goods and services, ready to be used, bought, and sold, not just by corporate giants, but millions of small to medium-sized businesses and organizations like yours.

The most commonly patented AI technology is *machine learning*, which frequently relies on "deep learning," "neural network" algorithms. The number of machine-learning patents has lately grown 175 percent per year on average. You need to know what these are and how they work.

This section will explain how these algorithms work, without getting too wonky about the computer code or math involved.

THE MATH OF AI

As we said in the introduction, AI is software at work on computer hardware, and it performs sophisticated statistical analysis of your digitized data. AI is just math.

So let's start with the math. Now don't close the book!

I want to equip you against the torrents of numbers and statistical calculations coming from data scientists. I'll explain the essential principles and spare you the formulas. The math, in some cases, is centuries old, and computers do it all today anyway, but you as the human have to understand what it's doing, because it doesn't.

Remember that the goal is to obtain business value from your data. The terms below will empower you as you get to know AI tools and implement them in your organization.[2]

At the heart of it all is *conditional probability*, which is just a percentage. What is the chance that something is going to happen—or not happen—given what has taken place? For example, given the data, what is the chance that this or that transaction will occur? And these percentages are constantly changing. There is, for example, no set percentage chance that you might develop colon cancer for the duration of your adulthood. Doctors hawking colonoscopies won't show you that your chance of having cancerous polyps is not just the national average, but that average *adjusted over time* by your age, your weight, the prevalence of the disease in your family, your daily diet, your level of physical activity, the incidence of intestinal inflammation, whether you have already been checked and cleared once before, etc.

Netflix's recommendation system, a major part of its market success, is likewise based on conditional probability. Given the films you have seen and liked, what other films should be recommended to you? Your own viewing history, however, is a very limited data set. What about everyone else who liked the films that you liked? What other films did they like? Netflix's recommendations made for you are based on a vast range of data entries about people's viewing histories and many other factors as well. AI algorithms process that data, calculate, and update those recommendations for each user. Netflix paid $1 million in prize money for the algorithm model in 2008. The paper about it is available online for free.[3]

Conditional probability is a key component of the math-mix that allows AI to constantly update and improve its predictive calculations in just about every imaginable application. Many call it "personalization," but the software and hardware that calculate it could not be more impersonal.

Prediction rules are just mathematical equations that describe the relationship between input data and the calculated output. You can also call them *models*. The easiest example is your maximum heart rate, given your age. Subtract your age (the input) from 220, and you have your maximum number of heart beats per minute (the output). As you age, your maximum heart rate declines. Add more and more data points, and the prediction rules become necessarily more complex. They are the "patterns" that AI can "detect." When you "train" an AI system on a data set, and it "learns a pattern," that means that it fits the prediction rules to match the data inputs and outputs.[4] I'll come back to this idea with "backpropagation," below.

Regression analysis calculates the statistical relationship between variables, usually an input and an output. You've probably seen a regression graph before, perhaps many times. A picture is worth a thousand words.[5]

The line, expressed in a mathematical equation, is the prediction rule for the relationship between the X and Y data entries for each point. The best equation has the lowest average distance of all points to the line. This mathematical achievement comes from Adrien-Marie Legendre in 1805.

Regression analysis can be linear, showing the relationship between a dependent variable and an independent variable. If more than one independent variable influences a dependent variable, then "multiple regression" can show those statistical relationships in linear and nonlinear ways. We won't go deeper into the math.

But now apply the idea of conditional probability, and that is how real-time language translation works in computers. Which word or phrase in English, for example, is most likely to match a word or phrase in German, based on the vast data set of translated texts, and given what you have just written hitherto? Such a trans-

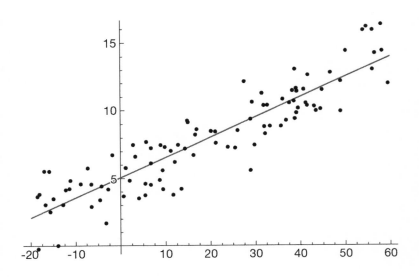

Figure 2.1. Regression Analysis *Source:* Public Domain. Wikipedia.org. Regression analysis. Image by Sewaqu, 4 Nov. 2010. Public Domain.

lation system is nowhere near perfect, because it has no idea what the words mean, but it is getting better all the time.

Parameters are just numbers that you can manipulate in prediction rules to obtain the best result. An example is 220 in your maximum heart rate (MHR) equation: MHR = 220 − Age. That number can move a bit based on the limitations of your data set. The more parameters you add, the better your model's accuracy becomes. MHR = 208 − 0.7 x Age is actually a better prediction rule. AI can handle many, many parameters, and they are essential for image recognition and identification. A certain model developed to distinguish between digitized images of two dog breeds has nearly 390,000 parameters.[6] No, you don't have to program or enter them from scratch. AI can set and adjust them automatically, based on the data sets used for training the model.

Bayes's rule (also called Bayes's law or theorem, or "Bayesian inference") only means that you have to update your current state of knowledge as more data becomes available. Bayes's rule is similar to conditional probability, and the basic idea is easy: prior probability + new facts = revised probability. The formula takes the prior probability that something is the case (a percentage), multiplies it by the accuracy of the new data (another percentage), which is then divided by the new data's results (a final percentage). (The actual formula is in this footnote.[7]) Thomas Bayes, by the way, is another oldie, a mathematically gifted English Presbyterian minister who lived and worked in the 1700s.

A good applied example of Bayes's rule is in self-driving cars. It is crucial for autonomous vehicles, drones, robots, and other devices to "know" where they are at any given moment, taking into account all the incoming sensor and location data. The vehicle's AI system must constantly calculate the need to adjust its position relative to other vehicles and potential obstacles (such as pedestrians), and even perhaps take evasive action.

A *vector* is just a set of numbers. Think of it as a horizontal row in a table with many columns. All the numbers in the vector are associated with the first in the first cell of the row. AI uses vectors to process language. AI "understands" human language by associating one word with others in numbers, ranging from 0 to 1. Think of it as the percentage chance that one word will appear near another. For example, "happy," generally speaking, has a low association (close to 0) with "new," but "happy" followed by "new" has an association much closer to 1 when typed at the end of December and the top of January, followed by "year." Happy New Year. The inputs of words and their "semantic closeness" expressed in numbers, compiled as "word co-location statistics," powers AI speech recognition: Alexa, Siri, Cortana, Google voice, and all chatbots.[8]

Variability is crucial for AI to identify statistical anomalies in data sets. Banks and credit card companies use it for fraud detection, and supply chain managers, forensic accountants, equipment maintenance managers, and sports teams apply it to data to predict when things may start to go wrong before a full breakdown occurs. The square-root rule specifies the average variability relative to sample size. You take the variability of a single measurement and divide it by the square root of the sample size. Formula One uses this to check streams of data from its cars' engines, tires, brakes, etc., to look for signs of impending failure. "Smart cities" use it to monitor and target inspections for many kinds of problems, from gas leaks to illegal subdivision of apartments.[9]

The constant threat of fraud in millions of electronic payment transactions demands the best tools for cost-effective, automated oversight. AI applications are cutting-edge, built on old math. The square-root rule was discovered by Abraham de Moivre in Switzerland in 1718.

See how there's little that's new in the math that underlies AI?! This chapter does not get into calculus, derivatives, and linear algebra, but they are even older, stemming from the 1600s. Without them, the algorithms you will meet next would be unthinkable.

THE SOFTWARE OF AI

Now for the software—the coded algorithms that perform the math.

You have probably heard the terms *machine learning, predictive analytics, deep learning*, and *neural networks*, which refer to groups of algorithms in code. We're going to go out on a limb here: In artificial intelligence, all four are pretty much the same thing.[10] Okay, "deep learning" algorithms are usually associated with image classification and voice transcription, but they use "neural networks" just like the others can. All four use the prediction rules or models discussed above. All four involve mathematical, statistical algorithms working on data. There's no need to parse technical jargon flaunted by marketers.

And, just to reiterate, machines cannot "learn" the way a human does; hardware and software are nothing like neurons; and "deep" can mean anything. Computers do not have self-awareness, independent consciousness, feelings, or even thoughts. AI software is a set of data-analysis tools. All code is prone to bugs, and all computer systems crash from time to time. AI is down-to-earth.

One final observation before we get to term definitions: Software is a lot like the law. They both find commonality in reason. Our point is that business software and the law are not natural enemies. Software and math classify and perform procedures—the former, with numbers, the latter, with words.

Indulge a shallow dive into distant history: The same person, Gottfried Wilhelm Leibniz (1646–1716), developed calculus at about the same time Isaac Newton devised mechanical calculators and created the binary number system that computers use today, whereby all numbers are expressed in 1s and 0s. Leibniz also developed a rational, legal "machine," a code, for classifying disputes (input data) and generating rulings (classification outputs). For him, math and the law complemented each other.

Okay. We're ready for the software.

Data captured in software must be accurate, reliable, and correctly classified for any of the above procedures to produce useful results. Computer data can come from many sources: keyboard entries, audio recordings, visual images, sonar readings, GPS, document files, spreadsheets, etc. The devices gathering sensory inputs must themselves be of high quality for the sake of accuracy. All the data is reduced to series of numbers and are normally stored in tables, with many rows and columns. If the data is flawed in any way, the procedures will be risky at best. If the procedures are inaccurate, then your business may make poor decisions and follow wrong actions.

As we said before, "Garbage in, garbage out" is as true today as it ever was. An AI firm proclaiming that its products or services can take any kind and quality of data and turn it into perfect predictions and decisions is just alchemy from the Middle Ages. Many people tried in vain for many centuries to turn common metals such as lead into gold. Even a genius like Isaac Newton poured many hours into that total waste of time and energy.

"Garbage in, garbage out" is true of the law as well. If the evidence is faulty or fake, the results of the court proceedings are going to be skewed, distorted, or just dead wrong. The goal is to calculate right determinations and benefit stakeholders. Data science and the law are compatible, indispensable tools in the struggle to make the right move and do the right thing.

Structured data refers to data stored in tables of rows and columns and formatted in a database for queries and analysis. Queries retrieve data, update it, insert more, delete some, and so on. SQL (structured query language), a computer programming language from the 1980s, is still widely used, especially by Microsoft and Amazon Web Services (AWS), and there are dozens of others. Structured data has to be clean and complete. It has to be accurate.

Let's use the 80/20 rule here: 80 percent of the time spent on your AI projects will be spent in data preparation. (More on that in chapter 5.)

AI guru Andrew Ng says that structured data "is driving massive value today and will continue as companies across all industries transform themselves with AI."[11]

Unstructured data gets more of the media attention, because people are more impressed when a machine can identify objects in pictures and respond to written and spoken speech in a humanlike way. Unstructured data includes digitized photographs and video, audio recordings, and many kinds of documents that people can readily understand much faster and more thoroughly than a computer. It took years and many millions of images and dollars to get AI algorithms to identify cats in photos with a high degree of reliability. Your average three-year-old child would get it right for the rest of her life after one or two encounters.

Back to data in general. It is the source of your organization's knowledge, not the AI. It is a key part of your institution's historical record, actually. Your data is a cross between a gold mine and a swamp. Working through it can really pay off, but you have to be very, very careful. Always maintain a healthy, skeptical attitude toward your data. How accurate is it, really? How was it compiled? Are there obvious or hidden biases that might skew your analysis and its conclusions?

Historical data presents a big problem for AI applications in the US criminal justice system. More often than not, inmates with lighter skin in the past have received parole at a much higher rate than those whose skin is darker, and it is no surprise that AI predictive models recently put these results into use in similar decisions.[12] To what extent does data about past court decisions reflect poor legal representation in court or base prejudice instead of actual guilt or innocence? There is no easy answer to this loaded question. Drug enforcement efforts quite frequently concentrate on neighborhoods with darker-skinned, poorer inhabitants, although drug trade and use are relatively color-blind and prevalent among all socioeconomic classes. Data collected from these efforts used to predict the best time and place for the next drug bust are virtually guaranteed to continue the trend. The computer certainly hasn't the foggiest idea that anything could be wrong in the data's origin or derivation.

The problem is nearly universal. In the United Kingdom, a model was used in Durham, in northern England, to predict whether a person released from prison would commit another crime—until people noticed that to a high degree, it correlated repeat offenders with those who live in poorer neighborhoods. Authorities then removed residential address data from the system, and the resulting predictions became more accurate.[13]

People are just people. We are sometimes rational and sometimes not, depending on the circumstances. If only our legal systems were as rational and reliable as mathematical analysis. The two meet in data and the analysis of it. Our great, shared challenge in this age of AI is that the machines serve the people, and not the reverse.

Let's return to our key term definitions for AI software.

Rules in software say what your organization will do with the outputs. You set the operational rules. You can have an AI system perform numerous tasks, but you and your organization, not the machine, are responsible for the results. Your rules must keep your organization's actions compliant with the law.

Will your chatbot or texting app use or suggest words associated with hate speech, however popular in use? Will you grant or deny credit to an individual? Will you interview this or that person for a possible job? Will you grant an employee a promotion or not? Will you place this order or not? Will you call the customer about a suspected case of credit card fraud? Will you dispatch a squad car at that time and place? Your organization is completely responsible for the data source—did you obtain it legally?—for the data classification, the procedures, and the rules. The law bans discrimination against people based on race, religion, gender, sexual orientation, etc., *even if you made no such data entries*. Other laws protect personal privacy about certain topics. (Joshua will explore this topic further in chapter 6.)

Scorecards set up the different factors that contribute to a complex prediction, such as the likelihood of whether someone will contract lung cancer, and algorithms working through masses of historical examples assign points to each factor that accumulate into a final score. Age and the incidence of the disease in family history tend to count more than gender, smoking more than income level or education. Because the computer calculates without thinking rationally, it can point out statistical relationships among the factors without any prior expectations. It may detect possible connections that health experts had not thought of. A computer does not bother with the distinction between cause and coincidence, so some of the correlations might prove medically absurd. (Recall the statistical connection between a person's IQ and their shoe size!)

Decision trees are used to model predictions based on answers to a series of simple classification questions. Using a breast cancer example, routine mammogram results divide patients into two groups. Those with no abnormalities are classified in the negative; the others go to the next question based on a mammogram. Were the mammogram results suspicious? The "no" answers are set aside, and the "yes" answers move on to the biopsy. That test may result in either a nonmalignant cyst, or, in case of a "yes," a recommendation for surgery and chemotherapy. To a certain extent, medical professionals are trained to think in decision trees—as should AI systems in the same field, no?

In AI, decision trees can manage multiple sources of data and run constantly. They can "decide" whether a vehicle accelerates, cruises, or brakes; turns left, turns right, or heads straight; remains squarely in its lane or heads to the side of the road to take evasive action.

Neural networks are a key component of most AI systems, but the term is fundamentally misleading. Recall the table about the differences between human brains and computers (see introduction). Neural networks are computerized functions performed by software on hardware, nothing else. They take digitized data, make many calculations quick as lightning, and end in a number. A real neuron is a living human cell that accepts and sends electrochemicals in the body. Human biologists actually don't really know how a neuron works, when it comes down to it. To compare a neuron to an electric transistor that is either on or off (reads either 1 or 0) is wildly misleading. But there is no point in trying to change the name at this point.

The best way to explain what a neural network in AI does is by way of example. Think of everything that can go into determining the actual price of a house at sale.[14] Square footage, lot size, year built, address, zip code, number of bedrooms, number of bathrooms, basement, floors, attached/detached garage, pool, facade type, siding type, window quality, inside flooring, family size, school quality, local tax burden, recent sale price of a house nearby, and so forth. Those are the inputs. For simplicity's sake, let's say there are thirty of them in a single column of thirty rows.

The neural network sets up an inner "hidden layer" of calculations—imagine another column of say, ten rows—in which *each* of the original inputs is "weighted," or multiplied by a parameter (a number you can change) and results in a single, new output number. Think of the hidden layer as a stack of ten functions that push the house price up or down. One could be for, say, "curb appeal," another for "in-demand trend," another for "family fit," another for "convenience," etc. All thirty input data points are included, each weighted differently by a set parameter, in each of the ten processed inputs in this first hidden layer.

The next layer does the same as the first, adjusting the numbers from the first hidden layer further, bringing them closer to a final recommended price. The final output is the price number. The input data, the inner "hidden" layers, and the final output comprise the neural network.

Although the statistical calculations linking the layers can become very complex, to say the least, the computer performs them accurately, except where bugs intervene—and they can be fiendishly difficult to detect. Given enough data entries and enough hidden layers, neural networks can produce some very accurate calculations. Neural networks can have one, few, or many hidden layers. The more there are, the "deeper" the neural network.

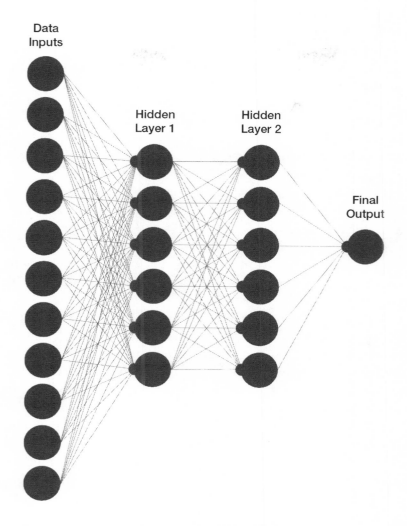

Figure 2.2.   Neural Network *Source:* **Image by Brennan Pursell**

"Deep" networks usually work better than "shallow" networks with fewer layers.

Here's the catch: The neural network has no way of knowing whether its output house price is accurate or not. It needs to be "trained" based on example data sets. You need to train it based on good data—actual examples, in this case, of houses successfully sold at a given price.

The beauty is that when you enter into the network the output and its matching set of inputs, the network's algorithms can adjust the parameters in the hidden layers *automatically*.

There are three key algorithms that make neural networks work. In them you will see that "deep learning" and "machine learning" really have a lot to do with training, but almost nothing to do with human learning.

Backpropagation makes the neural network adjust the weights in the hidden layers. Backpropagation is usually at the heart of "deep learning," "machine learning," and AI today. The algorithm was a breakthrough by Geoffrey Hinton and, independently, Yann Lecun, in the mid-1980s, although their work relied on research from the 1960s and '70s. Backpropagation only lately became an effective tool when available data and processing speeds both grew exponentially in the last decade.

Backpropagation starts at the output—the house price, in our example—and then works backward through the hidden layers toward the inputs. Say that the neural network predicted a price of $500,000 for a certain house, but you know that the actual price was $525,000. Backpropagation takes the correct price and adjusts the weights in each calculation in the hidden layers so that the neural network would come to the same price based on the initial inputs.

But that is just one example. If you train the network on many examples, then backpropagation averages all the adjustments that it needs to make, in order to optimize accurate performance across the entire data set.

The more you train it, the more you test its results, the better it gets.

Gradient descent refers to the mathematical process of measuring the adjustment of the weights—the parameters—in the hidden layers to improve the accuracy of the neural network's calculations and minimize the effect of errors in the data. Think of it as steps toward the sweet spot, the best set of weights in the network for generating the best, most realistic output, given the inputs. Gradient descent relies on derivatives in good old calculus, which determine the slopes of function lines.

Finally, the *sigmoid* and *rectified linear unit* (ReLU) functions help neural networks to generate clear "yes" and "no" answers and/or classifications (in the form of a 1 or a 0) or to sort data inputs into various categories. These functions are important in decision trees, as you might expect. ReLUs in particular enable neural networks to obtain their results faster.

"Recurrent neural networks," "convolutional neural networks," "deep belief networks," "generative adversarial networks," and even "feedforward multilayer perceptron deep networks" all rely on the software you just learned about. And none of them are worth anything without good quality data, and lots of it.

Equipped with the basic math and software underlying AI, you can readily face down any aggressive sales associate who tries to persuade you that his or her AI thinks like a human, one smarter than you.

As you have seen, the technical ideas behind AI have been around for decades, and their applicability in the workplace has soared in just the past few years. The amount of available raw data has exploded as more and more applications on more and more mobile devices collect data and share it on the Internet with service companies and their partners. We communicate and work increasingly through apps. The "Internet of Things" (IoT) is a volcano, disgorging data everywhere faster than anyone can measure. No one can stop it. "Smart" devices and sensors proliferate. Better hardware, from the individual device to the network systems, help to process and transfer that data faster than ever.

AI systems are increasingly capable of recognizing images, processing human language, and managing information in structured and unstructured data through statistical procedures. (I will revisit what applied AI can do for your organization in chapter 3.)

To sum it all up: Software and hardware put statistics on steroids—and it will get much, much more powerful over time.

We need to use AI because, when the data are well-labeled and the procedures are correct, computers run great numbers of them at high speed and low cost. Computers are also immune to human errors such as prejudice, favoritism, distraction, and mood swings (although we all wonder sometimes, when our systems suddenly slow down, freeze up, or crash).

Nonetheless, AI has three big problems: dependency, consistency, and transparency. *Dependency* refers to the machines' need for large amounts of high-quality, correctly classified training data. "Garbage in, garbage out," as we said earlier. *Consistency* is a problem because adjustments made to algorithms produce different end results, regardless of data completeness and quality. Different AI systems produce different results on the same darned data. Finally, and most importantly, *transparency* in neural network processes is limited at best. Backpropagation makes it extremely difficult to know why the network produces the result that it does. The chains of self-adjusting calculations get so long and complicated that they turn the AI system into a "black box."[15]

Despite these problems, AI functionalities are improving all the time, and applications of AI technology are proliferating in just about every sector of the economy. For every human being that uses a smartphone, there is literally no avoiding it.

3

AI APPLICATIONS
IN BUSINESS

AI BONANZA

AI is going gangbusters, and even the global COVID-19 pandemic can't stop it.

A research project by Microsoft in 2019 revealed that 38 percent of high-growth companies were actively working on implementing AI technology and solutions, while only 18 percent of low-growth companies were doing the same.[1] A report from *MIT Sloan Management Review* and the Boston Consulting Group found that 88 percent of businesses invested more in AI in 2018 than in prior years, and 91 percent expect AI solutions to add to their growth by 2023.[2] According to Wells Fargo, total revenues of tech firms exclusively devoted to AI will reach $202 billion in 2020, up from $130 billion in 2016. McKinsey Global Institute claims that AI will add 1.2 percent to annual GDP growth over the next ten years.[3] PricewaterhouseCoopers (PwC) foresees over $15 trillion in new wealth creation through enhanced productivity and labor savings in the same time frame. Some of these expectations appear to border on the hysterical, but the general consensus is unmistakable.

Governments across the world promote and support investment in AI technology, education, and application. In 2017 and
2018, the White House hosted AI summits to encourage American
companies to embrace this technology and integrate it with the
national workforce. The US military's tech research wing, the Defense Advanced Research Projects Agency (DARPA), will spend
$2 billion over the next few years on over eighty programs.[4] On
February 11, 2019, the US president signed Executive Order
13859, which highlights the need to train the workforce in AI
technology and to "foster public trust and confidence" in AI. In
2020, Congress was planning to allocate $100 billion to high tech
research, development, and commercialization.

Outside the United States, the British, French, and German
governments have recently poured at least a billion each of their
own currency into AI research and start-up support, but China is
the real powerhouse. The Chinese central government proclaimed
a strategy of "mass entrepreneurship and mass innovation," and
spent billions on AI start-ups and the supporting infrastructure.
Chinese local governments followed suit, adding to the mass national funding wave.[5] Fighting COVID only made it much taller.

Now add on private sector investment. From 2011 to 2018,
private equity firms, venture capitalists, and other corporate entities infused $50 billion in AI start-ups.[6] In 2019, total private
investment (not just in start-ups) nearly reached $40 billion in the
United States alone, $70 billion globally.[7] AI's share of global in-
vestment funding has quadrupled, from 3 percent in 2011 to 12
percent in 2018, the clear majority of it going to firms in the
United States, with China in second place. One firm in China,
SenseTime, having posted a 400 percent growth rate for the past
few years, raised $1 billion in three months to develop and market
its image analysis services.[8] In the United States, a single higher
education institution, the Massachusetts Institute of Technology
(MIT), announced a new $1 billion initiative in AI and computing
research and teaching, supported by a gift of $350 million from
Stephen Schwarzman, CEO and cofounder of Blackstone. Collectively, what Google, Amazon, Microsoft, and Facebook have spent

on AI research and development easily amounts to multiple billions of dollars. In 2019, Microsoft poured $1 billion into OpenAI, a nonprofit research center founded by Elon Musk, with the stated goal of achieving "safe artificial general intelligence."[9]

The current and permanent struggle for AI technology, however, is about profit. Some sectors, such as advertising, web search, and social media, have seen rich returns, while others are still waiting.

In spite of all the billions of dollars washing about, the gap in business readiness is vast. A study by Deloitte concluded that 90 percent of business and HR leaders across the globe recognized a paramount need to prepare for a digitized, data analytics future, while only 11 percent thought of themselves as well equipped for it.[10] Another Deloitte survey indicated that 47 percent of respondent organizations were working to automate repetitive tasks and enhance human productivity and performance using AI and robotics.[11] Expectations among business leaders that they will use AI in their organizations are on the rise, above 40 percent, although only 17 percent are knowledgeable about AI and its applications. In Germany, Europe's premier economic power, only 11 percent of companies reported the use of AI. The majority, however, believed that AI would play a key role in their country's ability to compete on a global scale.[12] The gap yawns wide, and audibly.

In such circumstances, firms intending to adopt AI must take caution: Every bonanza attracts snake-oil salesmen. A research project by British investment firm, MMC Ventures, concluded that 40 percent of the 2,830 AI start-ups do not actually use AI technology.[13] AI in this study is defined as "machine learning" algorithms that self-optimize based on current data. Too many start-ups say they are AI "focused," or working on dynamic implementation, whatever that is supposed to mean. Intentions alone do not guarantee actual results.

Always remember the spectacular rise and fall of Theranos as an instructive parallel. This story has nothing to do with AI but everything to do with mythical tech. From 2003, smart, young Elizabeth Holmes, all of nineteen years old, touted a new, wondrous technology that would have revolutionized health-care diagnostics. A drop of blood was supposed to reveal an individual's many health secrets. She teamed up with Silicon Valley high-roller Ramesh "Sunny" Balwani, raised many millions, and by 2013–2014, Theranos had a $10 billion valuation. She recruited illustrious bigwigs like Larry Ellison, Rupert Murdoch, George Schulz, Henry Kissinger, and Jim Mattis, all of whom bestowed their blessings on the enterprise while knowing precious little about the science behind it.[14]

These powerful connections helped Theranos to line up a large contract with Walgreens in spite of clear warnings from an outside technical consultant the firm had hired to perform due diligence, but the Walgreens management team's biggest concern was not to miss out on a potentially game-changing technology. They feared that an archrival like CVS would cash in before they did. Other fat contracts came from Safeway and the US military, supposedly. All along Holmes did not reveal her "proprietary" tech.

Touted benefits were smoke and mirrors. Theranos's magic machines never performed according to promise. Third-party vendors were used to fluff up test results. Holmes and Balwani mercilessly hounded out those who dared to raise questions, and lawsuits silenced them. The firm foundered, but the pair still managed to raise another $100 million in 2017. (Some deep-pocketed people with high hopes for massive profits catch on slowly.) The next year saw litigation, bankruptcy, and liquidation. Naturally the pair still maintain their complete innocence.

Theranos is just a one-company example in the highly liquid and profitable field of biotech. AI is a potentially game-changing technology trend, applicable in every major economic sector, and buoyed by a flood of money. Pirates and smugglers, inevitably, are out and about.

Until COVID, it appeared that the AI spending and investment bonanza might have peaked. Private investment in AI companies in China topped out at $4 billion in 2017. In 2018, it amounted to less than $2 billion. In the second quarter of 2019, Chinese AI start-ups raised a meager $140 million. Similar declines were noticeable in other markets. At the time of writing, the global fight against COVID caused enormous economic dislocation in the short term, but massive stimulus, investment, and human resilience will induce growth and progress to resume when the health risks are under better control.

Let's be clear about what AI can do now.

AI FUNCTIONS

Let's sum up what functions AI can actually perform for your business.

1. *Predictive analytics*. As described in chapter 2, these are statistical calculations that something will occur—or not occur—based on the given data. *Prescriptive analytics* relies on accurate predictive analytics. The former adds a recommended action based on the results of the predictive algorithm.

2. *Image or item "recognition."* In image recognition, computers associate arrays of pixel color numbers with text. They have no idea what or who is in any given picture, not the way a human does. Image "tagging" is a more-specific description of the programmed action. To us, it looks like the computer can say what is in a picture.

3. *Natural language processing (NLP)*. This phrase is yet another misleading marketing meme, as problematic as "artificial intelligence." A more-accurate phrase would be "human language tagging," but no one uses it in the AI services marketplace. Computers can process and predict words based on data about their occurrence in text files—that's all. An AI system, however, such as a chatbot, can associate words with processes, suggest text and e-mail replies, generate summaries based on word use in longer documents, and suggests translations from one human language to another. Add to that capability the transcription of voiced com-

mands. NLP can't manage a simple, free-flowing human conversation, but it is getting better and faster all the time.[15]

4. *Data transfers.* An AI system can survey reports and documents, associate numbers with certain words, and copy and paste the data from one application to another. All such tasks that are repetitive and do not need critical thinking could be automated, including basic financial and inventory reports, appointment schedule maintenance, basic steps in customer support calls, etc. Again, transcription of voiced commands can be added to produce something akin to a personal assistant, which will augment your people's productivity in the completion of their tasks.

5. *Content generation.* This is only practicable for computers to do within tightly defined limits and clearly scripted situations. AI cannot be truly creative like a human being. You have probably seen images of people and artwork generated by AI or heard music from the same. Given enough data, adequate training, and many rules and parameters, AI can certainly generate pictures of people with randomized facial features, hair color and cuts, and other contours. Music operates according to rules of rhythm, tonality, harmony, and structure. Music generated by AI should not bowl anyone over.

That being said, AI can certainly generate content in a number of forms:

a. *Text for generic SMS, e-mails, letters, debate lines, legal documents, basic journalistic articles, and even for simple comedy routines.* The more formulaic, the better, such as weather reports.[16] AI-generated jokes are usually horrible, however. Never expect a computer system, no matter how expensive, to develop a good sense of humor.[17]

b. *Text narration of video.* Such algorithms work through video—of a cooking lesson, for example—and associate the actions captured with written step-by-step instructions on how to complete the featured recipe. Textual accounts for sporting events coverage are made in a similar way.

c. *Audio files of music* in the popular and classical styles and graphics files of abstract and photorealistic images, both based on many, many examples.

d. *Movie trailers*, cut from the feature-length version—but don't vouch for their quality.

e. *Computer code.* Such AI programs can find free code pieces available on the web and arrange them to assemble a program that takes a specified input and generates the planned output.

Be very careful with all AI systems that generate text, audio, and video files from a database of digitized examples. Don't be fooled by dramatic marketing claims. Such systems cannot have a real sense of judgment. If AI programs are "creative" in the sense that they produce an audio or visual file that has never been seen or heard before, they tend to have irregular to very bad taste. It has been demonstrated time and again that humans need to do the final edits in every case. AI can help in the legwork, in the first compilation, but trusting it with final product is very risky.

You have probably heard about or seen "AI deep fakes" in video and audio. When presidents Obama and Trump visited China, national Chinese television coverage in each case showed them speaking a sentence in Mandarin, which neither can actually do. AI can tag facial features from video and photo images and link them to the movements associated with speech. The same allows for vocal sounds to be used to form audio files of speech in different languages. The result is usually poor quality—it is much easier to get a talented human mimic to impersonate the voice of another—but the technology is still relatively new.

The Samsung AI Center and the Skolkovo Institute of Science and Technology, both in Moscow, developed an algorithm to animate a single photo to make it move and sound like video and audio of another person. "Talk head image synthesis," as they call it, will only improve with time and give us less reason to rely on the veracity of video content.[18]

Intentional misinformation can be defamatory and destructive. You have also probably heard of AI celebrity porn, where the faces of famous actors and actresses, pop stars and politicians, are spliced onto such scenes. Some vicious, resentful people have been known to do the same with the faces of their exes, sharing the smut online. More insidious is the use of such tech for government propaganda, "fake news," and incitements to violence. It has contributed to the recent mass slaughter of the Rohingya minority in Burma (Myanmar), and extrajudicial killings in the Philippines, Cameroon, and other parts of the world.

As we said before, there is no technology in human history that has not been used as a weapon against others. AI software is no exception.

But let's get back to business. Let's stick with the five functions that AI can perform.

Never believe the salesperson who says that their AI HR software can let you know how your people "really feel" based on video and text analysis. People are more adept at hiding or disguising their feelings than machines are at reading them. Never let AI buy your supplies or run your supply chain, but definitely use its data-transfer and predictive-analytics functions to ease the workload and enhance precision and efficiency. Never let AI diagnose anything on its own.

Although some vendors would love for you to believe that the AI solution they are selling will guarantee bigger profits, they don't. Massive returns on AI investments are anything but guaranteed. These solutions need to be well planned, embraced by your people, deployed well, and carefully governed. Good management practices such as we have come to know them are still firmly in place.

AI ACCESSIBILITY

So AI is a veritable bonanza, and the tech is very real, although it does not always live up to advertisers' promises.

Where do you turn to get an AI system working for your organization?

You have three main options: consultancies, in-house, or a specialized vendor.

Major consultancies such as McKinsey and Accenture will gladly provide you with prepackaged digitization and AI implementation strategies, at the cost of many millions of dollars. There are many other consultancies, large and small, that would love to compete for the same business. The big-brand consultancies have done their homework, know what is going on, and have enlisted thousands of supposed experts, but is their business model the best for your organization, your mission, your people, and your culture?

The fact that you are reading this book speaks volumes.

You could also develop your AI solutions in-house. Instead of paying vast sums for a lead consultant backed up by college and MBA graduates, you can build your own AI team and use the platforms offered by software companies in the cloud. Or, in order to protect your proprietary IP from cloud computing pirates, you could equip your in-house team with the necessary software and hardware to do the job.

Or you could turn to a specific AI vendor with the solution that best fits your specific needs. You really don't have to reinvent the AI wheel, and you don't have to pay someone a mint for telling you how to use one. A wide range of ready-to-train AI software solutions are at your disposal. The best, most up-to-date list of AI vendors, at the time of this writing, is the website for Applied AI, https://appliedai.com, with over three thousand entries.[19] The list is long, but it's well organized by sector and relatively easy to search. Some of the vendors that appear in it are probably frauds, which is why you definitely need an expert to have a peek under the hood at the code. And, as a general rule, the more exaggerated the marketing rhetoric, the more intense the rat smell. And really, you may do quite well enough on your own.

Yes, you can. It doesn't matter how small your business is.

A farmer in Japan spent $1,000 for a homemade AI machine that sorts cucumbers according to the sixteen degrees of quality, as regulated in Japan. The farmer's son assembled a simple conveyer belt and camera, and set up AI image analytics using Google's TensorFlow. The trained AI classifies the photos of the cucumbers based on those of the sixteen degrees in its modest database, and little mechanical arms along the conveyer belt push the cucumbers into bins depending on the selected degree for each.[20] That well-invested $1,000 spared the farmer and his family many hours of a dead boring job: picking up each cucumber, looking it over, assigning it one of sixteen degrees, and putting it into the correct bin.

This modest example should give you an indication of how simple an AI application can be, what a useful, worthy investment it is, and how prevalent AI is going to become in our working lives in the very near future.

AI CLOUD COMPANIES

If you want to develop your own homegrown AI platform for cheap, without a significant investment in hardware or specialized vendor software, then consider the cloud-based AI services from the big computer companies we all know so well. People sometimes develop passionate feelings, both positive and negative, toward these tech giants. The good thing is, there are just enough of them to make for a decent selection. Online training on their platform is free, and they charge you nothing to get started building your own AI system.

Microsoft

Microsoft's wildly successful cloud services platform, Azure, offers a "Machine Learning Studio" that you can use with a web browser.[21] No need for calculus, linear algebra, Python, or other coding language. You can drag and drop data sets and "analysis modules" to build an AI experimental model. Instructional videos explain how you obtain your data, prepare it, define its features, select the best learning algorithm, and put it to use to make predictions. The site is loaded with tutorials, clearly written instructions, and step-by-step work instructions, with plenty of screenshots that show you exactly how to use AI in simple projects.

Microsoft also offers Azure Machine Learning services to support data scientists and Data Science Virtual Machines for building analytical applications. For larger, industrial-scale data sets, Microsoft's Cognitive Toolkit provides AI models for rent. These more-advanced neural network algorithms can be used for speech and image classification purposes. The firm's virtual assistant, Cortana, uses this toolkit for processing spoken search and task commands.

Microsoft CEO Satya Nadella aspires to make Azure the platform of choice for business software needs. Microsoft has launched an "AI Business School" with online lessons for executives about AI tech, how to develop an AI strategy, how to use AI responsibly, and how to lead cultural change in their businesses so that they can be more friendly and open toward AI. Microsoft's school offers tracks of classes in how to develop a successful AI strategy in manufacturing, retail, health care, financial services, and government.[22]

And beyond that, the firm has been audibly beating the morality drum about AI. Microsoft launched a $25 million "AI for Accessibility" fund to help the disabled learn AI tech. It also initiated a $40 million program, "AI for Humanitarian Action," aimed at helping children, refugees, and the displaced. President Brad Smith raised eyebrows across Silicon Valley when he exhorted governing authorities to regulate the use of AI facial recognition systems for the sake of personal privacy, preferably via a bipartisan commission. Microsoft general counsel, Julie Brill, said that the company would extend the protections of the EU's General Data Protection Regulation (GDPR) to all users across the world.

We praise all efforts to make AI comply with the law and actively support personal privacy, democracies, free societies, and free markets.

Satya Nadella also declared that Microsoft does not use its customers' personal data for profit. "We don't want to over-monetize," Nadella said. "If anything, one of the things we've done is to make sure that the utility is maximized for the users."[23] Against cloud competitors Amazon and Google, Nadella attempts to entice enterprise customers to Azure with a loaded question: "Do you want your tech partner to be your competitor?"

Alphabet (Google)

Alphabet's Google of course competes in the same space, but with a different approach. Google offers many services at no cost, but as a user, you permit the firm to do with your data as it pleases. Google's stated mission is "to organize the world's information and make it universally accessible and useful." In fact, Google gathers information about its users and sells it to advertisers. Most of Google's 1+ billion users don't care about the privacy of their data, but for the sake of your organization's intellectual property, you might want to be careful.

Google's basic services in that sense do not come for free. Data about you will go anywhere in the world to just about anyone willing to pay for it. California's Consumer Privacy Act of 2018 (A.B. 375), in force as of 2020, compels companies like Google to disclose the "personal information" they collect about individuals and provide a way for them to access that data, stop its sale, or even delete it. That law, however, only applies to Californians. Don't expect Google to change its business model anytime soon.

Google has poured billions into AI research, acquisitions, and investment. They rebranded their "Google Research Division" as "Google AI," and rolled out "Google Assistant," a voice-operated, AI-powered software set to fulfill your search, scheduling, directions, and other requests.[24] The firm is working on the next phase, "Google Duplex," which is meant to anticipate your immediate and future needs based on your historical data patterns. It helps you to complete your e-mails with commonly used phrases and explanatory texts based on words you already entered in the text. "Google Lens" aims to give you more information about objects that come into view on your camera. "Google News" will feed you more of the news your reading behavior indicates that you like. Late in 2019, the company upgraded their search and ranking algorithms, which generate the vast majority of their revenue and profit, with natural language processing AI.

For your AI projects, Google Cloud AI offers pre-trained models in structured data predictive analytics, "natural language processing," foreign language translation, image classification, and video analysis, ready to go and customizable.[25] In addition to the build-your-own AI capability, there are prepackaged solutions for sale at Google, for team productivity, HR, recruiting, marketing, customer support, and sales support in the retail, education, finance, entertainment, government, and health-care industries.

Google Cloud costs nothing to commence, and you pay for processing services as you go. By way of raw computing power, Google will rent you a Tensor Processing Unit (TPU) to perform AI mathematical calculations in the cloud for a fraction of what it would cost if you purchased the hardware yourself, depending on your use. One pod of Cloud TPU provides up to 11.5 petaflops (11.5 quadrillion operations of fractional numbers, not just integers, per second) of processing power. At a low cost per hour, a rented Cloud TPU may be the best deal for predictive analytics of your data sets.

Above and beyond Google Cloud is TensorFlow, Google's signature product for building AI systems on a small and large scale. It is a sophisticated open-source platform for developing AI solutions for your organization. Although TensorFlow comes with tutorials and plentiful learning assistance, it is considerably more complex than Google Cloud. You will maximize the benefits from TensorFlow if you make sure that your people are well trained in it. Coursera offers multiple courses about how to use TensorFlow, and anyone can audit them for free.[26] Never waste money on paying for training available to everyone for no cost!

Companies large and small have built their AI systems on TensorFlow. A significant proportion of AI start-ups use it, and the enterprising cucumber farmer mentioned earlier developed his sorting system with it. The giant of ride-sharing, Uber, relies on TensorFlow for "Ludwig," Uber's free, open-source AI toolbox for people to build and test AI models without prior knowledge of code.

Google allows its AI customers to benefit from immense data sets, such as its Open Images, which entails millions of images, already labeled, and organized into thousands of categories. Another data set, ClueWeb12, draws on written content from 800 million web pages. Because of Google's business model, the scale of the data at its disposal is awesome. Recall that in general, the more complex and sophisticated your AI model, the more data you need to train it. In 2019, Google paid $2.6 billion to acquire Looker, a cloud-based data analysis and visualization service. Looker helps companies large and small to make sense of their data and extract basic business insights from it.

To say the least, Google's goal for AI is to surpass Microsoft, and Amazon.

Amazon

Amazon built its behemoth online retail business on AI algorithms applied to historic customer and enterprise data for anticipating potential needs, suggesting products, optimizing prices, and identifying ways to improve its immense supply chain and delivery system. Other AI algorithms navigate this vast firm in order to identify statistical anomalies and classify cases of potential fraud.

Amazon, like any good business, sells what it does best. Amazon Web Services (AWS) is a suite of cloud-based software services that run the gamut from analytics to storage, machine learning to gaming, from mobile devices to satellites, blockchain to robotics. It's a stunning array of capabilities.[27] There are seventeen services under "machine learning" alone, such as Amazon Rekognition for image and video classification, including facial recognition. Amazon Lex offers spoken language transliteration and automated response services, such as text bots.

Apache MXNet is Amazon's open-source framework for AI application developers, from newbies to professionals. The Gluon interface is designed for simplicity, and MXNet offers crash courses in how to use it. The Gluon Model Zoo lets you assemble your AI system from hundreds of pre-trained models. With Gluon, you can prepare your data, build and train a neural network, make predictions from a pre-trained model, and use the GPU (graphics processing unit) in your computer to run the system.

As in the case of Microsoft and Google, open your account with AWS and get started with their tools and training. It's Amazon: They've got everything, and at a competitive price scheme. There are no up-front costs. You pay for what you use. And you can draw on their tutorials, project, whitepapers, and trainings based on successful use cases. There is a reason why AWS is Amazon's fastest growing division, and it dwarfs all other competitors.

We should add a word of warning here: There are numerous stories of Amazon hosting a company's data in AWS and then offering a similar product or service in direct competition. Amazon's cultural ruthlessness is well known. A notorious Jeff Bezos slogan is, "Your margin is my opportunity." Exercise caution if your data entails intellectual property, business know-how, and other information that your organization holds dear.

IBM

IBM's Watson famously defeated *Jeopardy* champions in 2011. IBM has generously funded research on AI, and it makes available important articles about AI capabilities, applications, and hardware developments.[28]

For business customers, Watson is available to perform many of the services described above for Microsoft, Google, and Amazon. Watson offers a virtual assistant rather like Google, Cortana, or Alexa, a studio for building and training AI applications with the option to use standardized models, data management tools, text analysis, image classification, speech-to-text and text-to-speech conversion services, and language translation. While apparently not the favorite among AI beginners, Watson's pricing scheme has been rated as competitive, even if the package for your business has to be negotiated. You can get started for free.

IBM researchers have been working on computerized conversation analysis, and Watson claims to be able to interpret tone and emotional states in and through speech. But we recommend caution. To IBM's credit, its website for "IBM Cognitive—What's next for AI" quotes the clear warning from Margaret Boden, a leading AI scientist since the 1970s: "AI and computing have progressed tremendously, but the capabilities remain quite limited. I doubt that computing will ever fully replicate the potential of the human mind, certainly not within the next few decades."[29] If people have a hard time "reading" other people's emotional states or true intentions, given our ability to hide our feelings and dissimulate, then a computer will most likely never get there.

But IBM is pushing the boundaries of AI applications beyond the typical business data analysis arena. IBM researcher Chieko Asakawa is working on a program to assist the blind with voiced narration of their scanned surroundings as they move through it. Asakawa, herself blind since the age of fourteen, is a leading light for this accessibility technologies. Yet another AI-based cognitive assistant by IBM helps people in wheelchairs or with limited mobility to find elevators in public areas. Yes, AI can do so much more than merely predict your next purchase, or mouse click.

Cloud Storage AI

It makes perfect sense for cloud storage companies to roll out AI data analysis tools for their customers. When the amount of documents, files, images, videos, and data entries reaches a certain (rather low) threshold, human beings rapidly lose the ability to manage and assess their content. There are many cloud-based data storage companies, but not all are jumping on the AI enhancement bandwagon.

Box is leading the way, precisely by not trying to reinvent the AI wheel; rather, Box integrates with the giant AI providers. Box Skills include Google's Cloud Image API, IBM's Watson Visual Recognition, Natural Language Understanding, and document analysis, Microsoft's Azure Computer Vision for image content search and analysis, and Azure's voice synthesis.[30] Through partnerships, Box pulls together an impressive array of data tools that its institutional customers can use for their business purposes. Box Skills Kit adds basic AI machine learning tools provided by Microsoft's Azure, Google Cloud, and IBM's Watson. All the while, Box claims to maintain the data privacy and security of its customers.

Of course, Box is not operating alone in its AI integration play. For its OneDrive storage users, Microsoft offers a search feature that transcribes audio and video files. You can scan their time-stamped written content without having to view or listen to the video and/or audio. MapR Technologies has rolled out its MapR Data Platform to ease and enhance data scientists' work, and Cloudtenna, a file consolidator, released its DirectSearch to work on data in the cloud, stored in on-site units, and in applications both hosted and online. New start-up Paperspace offers storage, virtual machines, AI solutions, data integration, virtual desktops, and user management.

As data volumes increase every day, AI tools improve and proliferate; the natural spot to perform your data analysis will be right
where you store everything. AI is available for your organization's
data in many convenient, affordable ways!

Apple and Facebook

We don't recommend that you bother with Apple and Facebook.

Both mega companies use AI to support their own business
models, but Apple has yet to offer an affordable, easy-to-use AI-
as-a-service for tailored business solutions. It may in the future as
it expands its offerings in services, and places less emphasis on
premium hardware products.

Facebook has rolled out PyTorch, a framework of AI tools for
developers, but, in our opinion, the firm has not done enough to
earn the trust of any enterprise or business customer.[31] If you
value privacy, intellectual property, and the law, there are better
companies to use as your tech partner. Facebook is a Silicon Valley pirate.

Don't Forget the Hardware

So far we have covered the major cloud-based providers of AI
software, but hardware companies, such as Intel and NVIDIA, are
certainly not going to be left out of the AI bonanza.

For simple image classification projects, Intel rolled out the
Neural Compute Stick 2, a USB 3.0 thumb drive with AI neural
network algorithms preloaded on its Movidius Myriad X processor
inside, for $99. The chip is a vision processing unit (VPU), and can
compute at 4 teraflops and perform 1 trillion operations per second, the kind of power necessary for AI image classification procedures, such as facial recognition, object detection, on data
collected from drones, cheap and powerful little cameras like
Raspberry Pi's, some robots, and other domestic scale devices.
Intel's Neural Compute Stick 2 claims to perform eight times

better than its recent predecessor, and it can integrate with Microsoft's Azure and Google's TensorFlow AI cloud-computing services. You need to use a server to train your neural network, but the little device is strong enough to run it once it is trained. Similarly, NVIDIA sells the Jetson Nano, for the same purpose and price, and Google is rolling out its new Coral product to compete in the same space. These little devices can be used for simple AI applications but are not suitable for industrial deployment.

NVIDIA, meanwhile, will keep riding the AI wave in its production of GPUs. While the central processing unit (CPU) makes most software work in a regular computer, the graphics processing unit (GPU) was developed to speed up processing of digital image and video content, especially for computer games. GPUs are found in desktops, gaming consoles, mobile phones, tablets, and many other computer devices. The GPU, as it turns out, can also run AI neural network algorithms much faster and more efficiently than the CPU. NVIDIA, a leading GPU company, markets GPUs specialized for AI processing: AGX systems for self-driving vehicles, DGX systems for predictive data analytics, and its high-performance Titan V GPU, with 110 teraflops, 3-D stacked memory, and 21 billion transistors.

In any booming market, competitors jump in for a piece of the action. Intel has its Nervana Neural Network Processor product line of chips for training AI systems. Qualcomm is dutifully promoting its AI hardware for smartphones, following a vision to make AI ubiquitous. Samsung invested $22 billion in AI technology in 2019 and 2020 in a direct challenge to Intel and NVIDIA. Samsung is positioned to install AI hardware in their vast gamut of products, from smartphones to washing machines, if they see sufficient market for it. Chinese giants Baidu, Huawei, and Alibaba are developing their own chipsets. Word has it that Facebook, Google, and Amazon are all at it as well. If AI processing chips are going into every conceivable computing device, it would be crazy not to. They've certainly got the cash for it.

An exciting hardware development is Graphcore's "intelligence processing units" (IPUs), chips that intermingle over one thousand tiny processors across the data storage area. This design does not fundamentally change AI classifications and procedures, but it does speed up the calculations at a fraction of the energy cost. Much energy is saved on not having to transfer great swathes of data. Maybe I am wrong, but the IPU does not sound any smarter than the CPU or the GPU, but for AI processing, it certainly does sound like a more-efficient device.[32] IPUs are meant for cloud AI providers and enterprise grade data centers, not private consumers.

AI cloud providers, one could argue, are already shifting their own model back toward consumer hardware. Google promotes "federated learning," where presumably Pixel and other Android smartphones process some of the data collected on that device according to machine learning models downloaded from Google. The results are sent to a designated cloud data center where algorithms continue processing, supposedly to improve predictive capabilities, all the while making sure that no one user gets direct access to another's data.

Google's dream is for everyone to wear earbuds and eyeglasses that record data about everything seen, heard, and spoken, collected by and provided to Google. Google Glass already failed once but has come back again. Earbuds connected to smartphones via Bluetooth wireless technology can use Google's speech classification and pairing algorithms to translate from one language to another in real time. Starkey Hearing Technologies, situated near Minneapolis, makes and markets hearing aids with real-time translations from twenty-seven languages. Founder Brandon Sawalich predicts his company's products will provide customers with their own "personal assistant."[33]

But given the wide variation in word order and sentence structure across spoken languages, a live, second-by-second, perfectly automated and accurate word-for-word translation service is not going to happen. Human languages don't really allow for it. In German, for example, the verb frequently comes at the end of a sentence. An English translation would have to pause for that final verb before continuing with the rest of the sentence. Delays and lag time are unavoidable. Instantaneous translation of the world's languages into one another, powered by AI, is a pipe dream. So let's not light it up.

AI APPLICATIONS BY SECTOR

If you do not want to set up your own cloud-based or on-premises AI system for your organization, there are thousands of vendors who would love to sell you their diverse services powered by AI algorithms. Excluding the frauds, the vast majority of the legitimate services are based on AI functions that we have mentioned repeatedly in the book so far: predictive analytics, image or item "recognition," natural language processing, data transfers, and content creation. Many of these AI start-ups have actually built their businesses on the platforms offered by Microsoft, Alphabet (Google), Amazon, and IBM.

The next section of this chapter provides an overview of AI uses across the economy by sector, illustrated by example. As you read, think about your organization, the way it works, and how it might benefit from these examples, in the context of your own internal functions and market dynamics.

Marketing: Advertising and Sales

Marketing is a vast sector, especially when we use the term to include product development, distribution of those products, promotion, and pricing. It has been claimed that half of what we spend as consumers covers marketing costs.[34] In this section, however, let's look only at advertising and sales support activities such as customer relationship management (CRM) and brand campaign management.

Advertising, without a doubt, has been the most profitable arena for AI in the economy, and two companies, Alphabet (Google) and Facebook (the owner of Instagram and WhatsApp), receive more than 50 percent of all digital advertising expenditures in the United States. In 2016 and 2017, both companies secured profits between $10 and $20 billion. In 2018, Facebook pocketed more than $22 billion, and Alphabet, more than $30 billion. The cash reserves in their war chests could cover about a year or more of their operating expenses.

It's pretty straightforward. People in general are much more likely to click on banner ads and other links that take them to the content that interests them. AI predictive analytics applied to historical data calculate the likelihood that you will click on a given ad. Digital advertising firms gather, process, and sell data about your Internet usage as fast as you produce it. Firms tie your data to your friends'. Yes, people are more likely to buy the same goods and services as their pals. Advertisers pay by the click and at a premium to push to the top of your feed. AI algorithms continually optimize the accuracy of their predictions, as fast as you produce usage data. You get more individualized recommendations, and they get the cash.

Alphabet and Facebook are in the lead on this game, but Amazon is rising quickly, and others, such as Snapchat, are vying for a larger slice of the pie.[35] Pinterest, another contender, uses AI in a similar way, but goes a step further. Using image classification, Pinterest enables its users to click on items in pictures and get suggestions on where to buy it, with vendor link and price right there. Of course, this will not work for everything pictured on Pinterest, but you see the attraction. Pinterest spares you the nuisance of coming up with the right words for the search bar. Just click on what you see and like, and the AI finds the item for sale online for you.

Old-fashioned advertising was about getting information from the sellers to the buyers to increase sales. Obtaining information about the buyer was a time-consuming, expensive, difficult job. Internet usage has ended the imbalance. Buyers reveal vast amounts of data about themselves by the day. Sellers pay to reach out to the buyers statistically most likely to purchase their goods and services. The winners in the online advertising market are the best matchmakers. Executives from online auction giant eBay stated that AI has added $1 billion per quarter in 2018 in additional sales.[36]

The Internet advertising pie just keeps on getting bigger and sweeter every year, not just in the United States, but all over the world, as people turn from paper and TV channels for their content to digitized print and video via smartphone and tablet. Newspapers shrink in size and revenue, and cable TV is headed toward the rocks. Centennials—aka, Generation Z, those born after 2000—show severely limited interest in either. They are truly Internet natives.

For brand campaign management, AI tools can recommend target websites, the different kinds of screens the ads should appear on, and what times they should play. Algorithms calculate the maximum number of potential customers who are most likely to view your advertising content and find it appealing, given your campaign goals, the quality of information about your target market, and available advertising formats. These tools will help to inform your decisions about where, how, and when to place your organization's digital media ads. In short, you can increase the sales value that you get out of your marketing budget.

Adobe features Sensei, an AI tool to work through brand marketing data and make recommendations based on patterns that indicate a superior customer experience with the material. Adobe Analytics pulls in a wide range of data gleaned from the web to give users better insights about their customers' behavior in real time.[37] The calculations, however, will only be as good as the data they are based on. Always beware of the quality of "information" floating out there for free on the web. Where did it come from, who put it there, and what is it based on?

In support of sales, customer relationship management (CRM) software helps sales personnel to turn contacts into leads, and then into sales revenue. The three goals of CRM are to win new customers, increase the sales to existing customers, and extend the time duration that your customers stay with you. Customer retention is a constant concern for marketers. The cost of acquiring a new customer is inevitably and significantly higher than holding on to the one your business now has. But customers, whether in the business-to-consumer (B2C) market or business-to-business (B2B), have to be treated like people, like the real individuals they are. AI analytics can help marketers gain more insights on how to meet and anticipate their individual customers' needs, to keep them engaged and excited about your offerings. If you were to increase your organization's retention rate by 10 percent, the value to your business would be easily three or more times higher, with the passage of time.

CRM is a natural fit for AI analytics. Malcolm Frank, of IT outsourcing giant Cognizant, asserts, "Marketing without AI will be no marketing at all."[38] AI-powered CRM can assist marketers in their work to learn more about the customer's experience with products and services, and it can help sales teams move away from pure lead generation through cold calls and ill-prepared pitches. AI tech can augment the very human work of CRM for richer customer relationships and higher sales volume.

Two start-ups, Conversica and Tact.AI, provide CRM to their customer companies with a virtual, AI-powered sales assistant.[39] You pick the name and the work hours for the assistant, and it's never late and never calls in sick. Built on a database of millions of messages, a chatbot can reach out to potential leads according to their level of contact with the website and other parts of the target firm, using texts, chat windows, and e-mails. AI algorithms associate and recommend the messages that were used with other, similar leads that were converted successfully into sales.

People.ai is another competitor in this space, and they just raised $60 million in series C funding.[40] Sales and marketing virtual assistants handle the initial, easy, and tiresomely repetitive exchanges early in the relationship. They can schedule sales calls after a prospective customer has accepted that a bot will handle the task. Disclosure helps to develop a healthy working relationship. Routine follow-up calls are another possible application. Such AI products are meant to save a salesperson's most valuable assets: his or her time and effort.

The leader in cloud-based, software-as-a-service (SaaS) CRM is Salesforce. Salesforce's AI product, Einstein Analytics Platform, has been available and adding features since 2017.[41] Einstein works across Salesforce's whole platform to help with lead generation and prioritization, closing sales, automated chatbots for initial, simple customer service responses, marketing and sales predictions, and data-based purchase recommendations. Salesforce's partner developers can build customized apps for their clients that use Einstein's AI processing power. Salesforce also allows for Einstein to integrate fully with IBM's Watson for business intelligence. For beginners, Einstein comes with "Discovery Basics" for initial setup and training in data queries (aka, "create a story"). The visualizations of data are clear and straightforward, and in 2019, Salesforce paid $15.7 billion to acquire Tableau, a premier data visualization and presentation software solution. With AI analytics and Tableau, Salesforce is in an excellent position to maintain its leadership position in SaaS CRM.

The advertising sector, brand management, and CRM are all blazing hot markets for AI applications. SAP, the business software giant based in Germany, snapped up Qualtrics International for $8 billion in cash, a price 75 percent higher than its planned IPO valuation. Qualtrics, founded in Utah, specializes in surveys and interpretive software to help manage customers, employees, brand, and products.[42] SAP wants to give Salesforce a run for its money in CRM by integrating this function with its long-standing strength in supply chain, financial management, and enterprise resource planning (ERP) software.

Customer Support

We have all been there: stuck in an endless, idiotic phone tree without the option you need, a trap system deaf to your pleas for help or customer service or any sentient human being. Some are so bad that it seems the company wants their customers to drop service instead of fixing their problems. And then there are the chatbots. You go to the good or service provider's website, register and open your account, go to "help," and are faced with a grinning pop-up chat box that has no idea what your issue is or how to solve it. You write short phrases or sentences and receive answers about a completely different matter.

In spite of all that, automated customer support is here to stay. The good news is that it is getting better, now faster than ever. In fact, you should expect a rise in the use of chatbots that work with customers, and with each other, to get simple customer support tasks done because of AI-powered natural language processing. Furthermore, people need to touch the keyboard less as real-time language transcription is improving in quality and capability all the time.

Not that any computer can "understand" human language the way we do, but AI algorithms can take audio data, break it into parts according to phonemes, and arrange the breaks into words according to probability, given the situational context and the task at hand. The simplest tasks—those that require no critical thinking, like looking up an account balance, listing recent transactions, arranging for payments, and refilling prescriptions—can be done by computers alone, as we all know. Increasingly, they can take orders, set up appointments, and channel a range of customer service issues.

In order to reduce mind-numbing repetition for human workers, we recommend that your organization seriously consider use of AI applications to field calls and process requests at a basic level. Such software could be used to authenticate users for basic access to the given system in order for them to obtain the least risky information that they need. As customer needs rise in complexity, so does business risk: Failure to satisfy the customer throws open the exit door. The work of ticket creation and case routing can be enhanced by AI, but a human should oversee it according to business risk assessment.

Case escalations should be readily available to people that the system cannot correctly and reliably serve. AI analytics can help to predict those cases most likely headed for escalation in real time.

And when a case is handed from the chatbot to the human associate, all the data of the interactions with the chatbot ne'd to be
presented to the human so that the poor, annoyed customer does
not have to start all over again with self-identification and description of the problem.

The name of the game in customer service automation is personalization. Excellent customer service is about excellent communication with the customer as a person. Customers need to
know that their business matters to the firms that serve them.
Apart from gigantic Adobe in Silicon Valley, smaller companies
are charging into this business space across the world, such as
Dynamic Yield, LivePerson, and Monetate in New York; Evergage
in Somerville, Massachusetts; and Certona in San Diego and London. This application of AI tech can help satisfy your customers
and retain them.

For businesses and organizations with global reach and an
international customer base, real-time foreign language translation
is another terrific AI-powered service that is getting better all the
time. Such algorithms match running strings of words and phrases
to the most probable equivalent in another language. In a specific,
narrow context of a scripted business task, such as a customer
service interaction, AI algorithms can determine the most likely
parallels in other languages at high speed with appropriate accuracy. Of course, written text is easier to process, but spoken language only adds another step in translation processing. As said
before, while real-time translation is currently out of reach, it has
come into view on the horizon. Maximizing this capability will
enhance the personalized experience for customers across the
globe.

According to Igor Jablokov, the future of work—and, you could
argue, of customer support—lies in speech, not typing on a keyboard. Jablokov founded Yap, a speech recognition company, and
sold it in 2011 to Amazon, which uses the tech in Alexa and Echo.
The only AI product that matters, he proclaims, is "accuracy."[43]
Expect to see speech-enabled AI virtual assistants proliferate, in
homes, business, and customer support lines and websites.

Medical

With or without a pandemic, the medical industry in the United States is a cost monster. Spending $3 trillion a year, it dwarfs advertising by a factor of fifteen. As of 2018, health care devours 18 percent of the US GDP, and it gets hungrier every year, even as US public health ratings stagnate or decline. The same trend is discernible in other advanced economies around the world, but it is particularly pronounced in the United States. Government regulators want to cut costs and improve quality, which is a tall order for anyone, but especially for regulators. AI technology can help, and spending on AI solutions for health care may grow 48 percent per year, to reach $22 billion in 2023.[44]

We probably all have experienced waste and inefficiency in medical overhead, whether in doctors' offices, hospitals, insurance paperwork, flexible spending accounts (FSA), health savings accounts (HAS), etc. AI applications could make major cost-saving contributions to automating the scheduling of appointments and the check-in and check-out procedures. Athenahealth, a medical services company that has adopted AI to tackle this immense and obvious problem, estimates that $91 billion per year—this represents 14 percent of all medical spending—is squandered on antiquated medical overhead.[45]

Record-keeping and data transfer are major headaches for medical providers, because regulators, despite good intentions, impose hindrances. The law guarantees the portability of patient data from one health-care provider to another, but unfortunately, it is still tied to the venerable fax machine. In Athenahealth's customer network alone, 100,000 service providers send 120 million faxes per year. Fax machine numbers are publicly listed, so unwanted advertisements routinely burden these machines.

The biggest problem is that fax machines do not send text as structured data, so they actually hamper the flow of information from one service provider's computer system to another. Test results, reports, prescriptions, and other documents sent this way have to be read and their data either re-keyed or filed one way or another. Athenahealth uses AI to read the text on faxes, sort out the high-risk cases, and schedule appointments for them automatically.[46] We can only hope that regulators will one day update technological requirements to free us from faxes. In order to give proper advice, doctors need full and unimpeded access to all information about their patients' health.

Another problem is that the raw amount of health-relevant information is growing faster than anyone can manage. Smartphones, smartwatches, Fitbits, internal monitors (such as pacemakers), and every other external monitoring device can potentially gather basic biometrics around the clock. Showing up at an appointment and getting your pulse taken gives the doctor one data point when, in many cases, whole databases are available for analysis in ready charts and other presentable formats. Alphabet's life sciences company, Verily, is working on holistic care management based on the full range of data.[47]

AI predictive analytics applied to available data will improve preventive medicine, and the range of available data has moved beyond the confines of regular, regulated, medical data. Eric Horvitz at Stanford University includes people's Internet search terms in his databases and claims to improve the accuracy of predicted diagnoses of Parkinson's disease and pancreatic and other cancers. He surmises that people are more likely to search the Internet about their symptoms before they actually contact a physician. He calls his AI-powered solution "health-related sensing at large scale."

To Horvitz, accessing search histories is like listening to "the whispering of millions of minds." Combined with normal medical data, he claims that his algorithms help doctors to identify disease earlier and more accurately. In the case of Parkinson's, he even includes mouse-tracking data "as a digital proxy for a tremor" in the hand and arm.[48] Some have criticized Horvitz's approach as akin to a doctor using gossip to diagnose, but he remains undeterred. The statistical results speak for themselves. Correlation is not causation, but it can help.

To say the least, medicine in our world today needs AI, for data analytics. But let us be very clear: No one should have a goal to replace physicians, but rather to aid them in processing the information they need to make the best diagnoses possible for their patients and improve their treatment outcomes. AI can help make medical personnel more precise and efficient in their work. No algorithm can serve as a true physician. If AI natural language processing can produce an accurate, reliable voice transcriber, trained to each doctor's voice, for taking notes and filling out forms, then that tool alone would allow doctors and patients to look each other more in the eye than on the screen. In that sense, AI might help to humanize the reigning medical industry.

AI uses in the health sector abound. Sensely's "Molly" serves as a virtual health assistant. Woebot provides psychological monitoring. Semantic Scholar educates patients about their conditions. HeartFlow data analysis claims to diagnose heart disease more accurately than coronary CT angiography. Butterfly iQ is a personal ultrasound scanner that fits in your pocket and shows its results on your phone. PatientsLikeMe is a site for crowd-sourced post-diagnosis information and support. Noom will predict your weight loss if you follow the program it recommends.

What happens in most doctors' offices? People check patients into record-keeping and financial systems, other people gather patients' immediate and historical data, and diagnosticians analyze the data, classify the problem, and prescribe treatment. What if patients checked themselves in? What if data collection was semi-automated, and cumulative data were presented to diagnosticians with structure and analysis? What if patients were monitored and informed to take better care of themselves?

You could fill a book with medical AI applications alone. Below are just a few to give you an idea of the potential range. AI can:

- Automate note taking and record entries for doctors in medical examinations
- Power chatbots and virtual health assistants that help patients to manage their symptoms, data, and appointments

- Scan a patient's medicines, flag contraindications, and rate probabilities of medical connections among all the symptoms, whether or not they are the immediate concern of a given specialist
- Determine whether or not a patient will fill a prescription and potentially incur complications from not following doctors' orders[49]
- Perform early cancer diagnosis from predictive analysis of cell-free genomes floating in the blood. Why wait for an expensive tumor biopsy when a blood test might do?
- Classify images of the retina, the lungs, the heart, areas of the skin, and really, any part of the body according to possibility of early signs of certain medical problems[50]
- Use voice and breathing patterns from emergency callers to assist medical dispatchers to assess danger of heart attack[51]
- Use self-balancing, semi-autonomous mobile exoskeletons to help paralyzed patients to walk again safely
- Provide voiced narration of local surroundings for the blind[52]
- Calculate the risk profile of new drugs at a higher level of accuracy and so speed up their development and cut their cost
- Determine a woman's fertility real-time based on her current body temperature[53]
- Scan electronic health records and data and predict who is most likely to attempt or commit suicide before depression and despair drives them to that point
- Apply the text analysis algorithms to young people who text crisis hotlines to classify them by severity of need
- Enable hearing aids to track temperature, daily number of steps and stairs, amount talking and interaction with others, heart rate, and fall detection[54]

AI is the present and future of medicine. Costs spiral higher at a completely unsustainable rate, and combined with long life expectancy, declining birth rate, rising obesity with all its attendant health problems, and proliferation of expensive new drugs, treatments, and technologies, something has got to give. Government regulators will slow progress, but won't stop it. They cannot afford the political costs of the majority of their populations pushed toward financial ruin after a single accident or mishap.

Assisted living for the elderly is closely related to the great medical mix. Their numbers constantly increase worldwide along with economic growth, and everyone breaks down the older they get. Eventually, pretty much everyone is going to need some help. Cera, a firm based in the UK, gathers digitized data about potential patient characteristics as well as that of available caregivers for optimized care.[55] Elderly people in different living situations are analyzed to predict the likelihood of a malady and are then paired with caregivers for early intervention. Cera draws on a wide variety of data points in addition to purely medical data, such as what languages people speak, whether the elderly live alone or have pets, etc.

According to Ben Maruthappu, Cera's CEO, "Our system can predict the risk of deteriorations in patients—the risk of a fall, the risk of a hospitalization. This means that as we get bigger we can see which patients are high risk and which ones are low, and therefore who needs more care and who doesn't. And this again allows us to be much more proactive."[56] The key to this business, however, is quality of care, not just good data analytics. Cera also gathers and analyzes information about caregivers' punctuality and performance. Automated, round-the-clock monitoring of both patients and their helpers is a valuable tool to protect people as they age, and inevitably weaken.

In 2019 the British government allocated £250 million to set up a National Artificial Intelligence Lab to enhance disease prediction, prevention, and treatment and reduce administration costs in the country's National Health Service. They expect better and faster screening test results for multiple kinds of cancers, eye diseases, and heart problems. The goal is to manage and schedule more efficiently the country's hospital beds, treatments and procedures, medicines, and medical devices.

Finance and Insurance

A report by Autonomous Next claims that AI technology will cause a major shakedown in the cost structure of the $1 trillion financial services industry. The authors believe that 20 percent savings can be achieved overall, from the back to the middle, and on to the front offices. A whopping 2.5 million jobs might be "changed" in some way by AI applications. In the front office, they foresee a tighter integration of financial data and account actions, supported by chatbots that can manage communication channels with clients. In the middle office, AI systems can help with oversight of regulatory compliance and risk management. And, at the back end, AI systems will take over credit risk calculations and improve them by incorporating social media and other data about a potential customer's Internet presence and profile. The same can apply to insurance underwriting and claims assessment. All this, they claim, applies to banking, investment management, and the insurance business.[57]

Will robots replace financial advisors? Only if people are crazy enough to rely exclusively on their calculations. Will algorithms decide all trades in equities and securities? Only if we ignore history and are fool enough to let them. Purely quantitative solutions have been applied to the markets before, with spectacularly bad results. Long Term Capital Management (LTCM), founded in 1994, relied on brilliant algorithms for derivatives pricing that earned the owners a Nobel Prize in economics, but their training data set only went back five years, missing the last time when all market indices plummeted. The hedge fund generated enormous profits for a few years until the Russian government's default in 1998 induced a panic. LTCM, in spite of its Nobel laurels, lost its billions in a matter of months.

Here's a big but obvious claim: No machine can accurately predict or explain an individual human being's psychology—people's thoughts, feelings, motivations, dispositions, strengths, and weaknesses are just too complicated—so machines can't do so on a mass scale. Markets are as rational and irrational as people. Markets have no independent agency. They are large-scale expressions of human behavior, which is why they surprise us again and again. We surprise each other. Yes, financial markets these days are arguably dominated by a handful of enormously wealthy institutional investors, but if large numbers of their clients put in sell orders, they will have to follow suit.

Neither people nor computers can regularly pick the optimal time either to invest or to cash in and head for the door. The dot.com bubble and bust (1995–2002) and the great financial crises of 2008 and 2020 are cases in point. In each, a lucky few nailed it, such as Bill Ackman, whose COVID pandemic hedge bet earned $2.6 billion. But those that claim AI will demystify finance, I fear, are trying to build castles of profit on air, until the winds change, as people inevitably make them do. Data and algorithms won't end human history's unpredictability.[58]

AI cannot adequately or reliably explain the dynamics of greed and fear in any one individual, let alone all participants in a national or global economy with disposable wealth. Booms happen when people invest above the usual rates. Bubbles develop when people continue investing despite indications that those investments will not generate commensurate profits. Busts occur when people stampede to clear out.

That being said, a hurricane is building for the financial services industry, and for its job structures. Virtually all tasks in a financial business that are quantitative and repetitive may be subject to alteration because of AI, from mild increase in productivity to outright automation and elimination. Below is an overview of notable start-ups and established companies using AI to provide financial services:

- Stripe is an extremely well-funded cloud-based payment services firm that speeds up credit card and bank payments. Its fraud protection product, Radar, uses AI to analyze data points related to a given transaction and assign it a fraud rating. Stripe claims to reduce fraud instances for its business clients by 25 percent. In one year, it flagged $4 billion

in fraudulent transactions, limiting the losses to its clients.[59]
If Stripe continues on its trajectory, it may challenge the
world's largest banks in the electronic payment space.

- Affirm aims to upset both the credit card and the credit
  scoring industries. The company uses its own AI algorithms,
  not the FICO score, to rate customers and issue them credit
  quickly, nearly on demand.[60] While its interest rates are certainly higher than those of bank loans, Affirm makes its re-
  payment terms clear and simple. An increasing number of
  stores accept payments from Affirm's app as though from a
  credit card.
- Black Knight Financial Services, which provides work flow,
  data, and analytics software solutions for real estate and
  mortgage companies, acquired AI start-up HeavyWater to
  help expedite loan origination and servicing through automated verification of income, assets, and insurance coverage.[61]
- MindBridge has developed an AI-powered platform to enhance and automate aspects of the audit process. When it's
  fed accounting data, it can apply a risk score to transactions
  and flag those for the auditor's critical scrutiny.[62]
- Overbond forecasts price ranges for corporate debt and predicts the likelihood and timing of companies issuing bonds.
  Such information decreases the need for investment bank
  services.[63]

Among financial AI start-ups, Upstart Network does roughly
the same tasks as Affirm, but for personal loans specifically, not
payments to retailers. ZestFinance offers machine learning algorithms to optimize credit underwriting. Fraugster, a German-
Israeli start-up, aims to slash the incidence of online payment
fraud by as much as 75 percent, issuing a score or an automated
decision in as few as 15 milliseconds, and YayPay aims to increase
the efficiency and effectiveness of businesses' accounts receivable
(AR) collections.

The big banks—Bank of America, Citigroup, Wells Fargo, JPMorgan Chase, etc.—sense the tremors beneath them in the "fintech" start-up landscape, and they are all investing in AI systems and chatbots to serve basic customer needs, and to flag signs of ethical violations, bias in lending, fraudulent activity, cybersecurity violations, and the like. The question is to what extent community banks and credit unions will be able to keep up with the competition. When the seas rise, nothing set on the nearby, low-lying land is truly secure.

The insurance industry offers many exciting possibilities for AI applications to speed up claims processing. Ping An Insurance, one of the leaders in China, for example, uses AI to classify images of cars damaged by accidents in terms of severity. Customers take a photo of the damaged vehicle and submit it to the company via an app. The AI application compares the photo to those in the company's database and assigns a reimbursable sum. Ericson Chan, CEO of Ping An Technology, the tech arm of the Ping An Group, says, "Before . . . your car gets towed away, we can immediately reimburse the money back into your account."[64] Obviously, the photo will not capture the damage done to the car that cannot be seen, but for those customers who value speed over accuracy, convenience over caution, this insurance solution is optimal.

Travelers Insurance uses the drone-operating company Kittyhawk to survey areas flooded by hurricanes, a step that greatly speeds processing of claims adjustments. Drones flew over portions of North Carolina after Hurricane Michael in 2018, recording flood damage to allow for faster claims adjustment.[65] Travelers has six hundred insurance agents who are FAA-approved drone pilots. The drones also record video at construction sites, for firefighting, and to provide evidence for law enforcement efforts.

On the consumer side, because of the welter of fast-moving, available data, the whole rhythm of one-time, annual insurance renewals may be headed for the door. Amodo can help car insurers to adjust rates based on real-time data about how their customers drive.[66] For risky teenagers, why base rates on age, short to nonexistent driving record, and grades in school when a "telematics" device installed in the car or an app on their smartphone can send a stream of information about how they actually behave on the road? If data reflect a cautious driver, then rates should go down; a maniac at the wheel, then they should skyrocket. This same idea and tech can be applied to truckers and cargo ships, given weather reports. How many Fitbit and Apple watch wearers would be glad to see their health insurance costs fall based on an optimal number of steps they walk each day and the number of times they exercise per week?

But in a world where everyone produces digital data, can health insurers know too much? Health insurers have been touting to one another the benefits of gathering "lifestyle" data as "social determinants of health."[67] But should your rates be allowed to rise, or should you be denied coverage if your insurance provider's algorithms tag your face in a series of skydiving photos posted by your friend? If you are photographed whitewater rafting without a helmet?

Regulators have their work cut out for them. In the new era of no privacy, legislators ought to define the kinds of data that insurers can use to exclude people from coverage or price them right out of the market, when they might be in perfectly good health. And each individual should have the right to know how decisions about their coverage were made.

HR

HR poses a real challenge. There are definite limits to what computers can tell us about human beings, and human resources personnel are obviously and principally concerned with an organization's most valuable resource: its people—from recruiting to hiring, on-boarding, training, performance reviews, promotion, conflict resolution, team optimization, skill development, and termination.

But much of the work is so repetitive, the expense so high, and the numbers of people in large organizations so great, that pressure to use cost-saving AI functions is nearly overwhelming. Strongly consider embracing the cyborg for HR tasks for your organization. Use the AI tool to supplement human work with other people, not replace it. The dream, for some, is to have a machine do human work, but it never will; not completely. Only people have a real shot of managing people, and that's hard enough as it is.

Some HR AI companies, however, promise extraordinary (that is, human) capabilities from their algorithms, such as "intuition," and even "emotional intelligence." While image analysis software has achieved very high rates of accuracy at tagging individual faces with names, and can do a super job at differentiating men from women in general, do you really believe that it can accurately assess a person's true feelings? There are hallmark signs of sadness in facial features and body language, but some people look that way all the time, regardless of their actual emotional state. Does anyone actually believe that the fixed, workplace perma-grin is an accurate indicator of real happiness?

The problem is not technology but truthfulness. You want to have people in your organization who truly want to be there. Job-hating people have higher rates of absenteeism, lower perfor-mance, and are more likely to leave, adding to the HR costs of finding a replacement. Most people can put on a happy face for the interview and manage their way up the firm's ranks, but what are they like when the boss or the HR manager is not there to observe? We all have met the coworker who is a honeysuckle with the manager but toxic with the people they manage. No mathe-matics, no matter how complicated, can solve the problem of hu-man duplicity.

That being said, AI entrepreneurs have developed HR virtual assistants to help with the workload, and their value-add is signifi-cant. The recruiting process is particularly slow and costly. Ac-cording to the US Bureau of Labor Statistics, hiring for a position takes nearly fifty days on average, and costs more than $4,000. TextRecruit's AI-powered chatbot, "Ari," announces jobs, screens candidates based on given criteria, and helps candidates to schedule interviews via SMS.[68] Hiremya.com's "Mya" and Paradox.ai's "Olivia" perform similar functions.

AI is best deployed early in the hiring process, as a chatbot for people to use to enter basic information about themselves, the jobs they seek, and their qualifications for them. They can also take a psychological quiz that gives an indication of how well they would "fit" the company. Your system should compare their results to those who left or failed at the job. That measure alone can reduce churn significantly. AllyO, which raised a total of $62 million and shows fast growth, uses chatbots to search for job candidates actively; to gather information about them and to screen and rate them; and to schedule appointments for people to meet them.[69]

For assessing current employee levels of job satisfaction and managing turnover, Ultimate Software's Xander analyzes textual responses to chatbot survey questions and connects them to other data about employees, such as attendance records and performance ratings. Xander tries to assess their emotional states, which then can be used to predict training needs, relationship remediation, and potential resignations.[70]

Xander cannot really "read" facial expressions, although the company's marketing video strongly implies as much. Xander conducts analysis of typed text. Of course, people can always write a response and mean something completely different depending on their emotions, but the point of the tool is to reduce the time that a team of people in HR spends reading the survey responses from hundreds or thousands of employees, citing risky cases, and comparing each to other company data on them.

In a survey-saturated, digitized society, people expect quick reactions to the data they provide. The data analysis and turnaround time on institutional responses to surveys need be kept to a minimum. The longer HR support takes to respond, the less relevant such data becomes to employees' actual emotional situations.

Large companies are leading the way with AI-enhanced HR departments. Unilever, a global consumer goods giant with over 150,000 employees in more than five dozen countries across the world, has been using AI in new-hire screening. Aided by Pymetrics and HireVue, candidates do not submit résumés, but rather connect the company to their LinkedIn profiles. If the algorithm determines a possible fit, Pymetrics gives them some games to play on their smartphone or tablet to measure their memory, their ability to focus, their risk tolerance, and their basic emotional intelligence.[71] If they perform adequately, HireVue conducts a video interview, and the system rates them based on word usage, voice intonation, posture, and facial expressions.[72] If they make it through these tests, they are invited to spend a full day at a Unilever office to test for fit and to meet key people. In thirty days, Unilever doubled its total applicants in North America. Their ethnic/racial diversity jumped, and they achieved a balance between women and men in new hires. Average hire time fell from four months to four weeks. Recruiters' productivity skyrocketed.[73]

On a smaller scale, for police departments specifically, Darwin Ecosystem aims to speed up an application process that can take months in some instances.[74] Rather than reducing requirements, this firm uses AI on IBM's Watson platform to analyze applicants' short essays (200 words) to draw conclusions about theirs skills and ethics.[75] The system doesn't bother with rules of grammar and syntax but rather with the incidence of words and phrases selected by the candidate. The data analysis associates the essays to the actual performance of past recruits in their first years, to those that succeeded, faltered, and failed. The intent is to supplement psychological exams in the recruitment process, not replace them, and Darwin Ecosystem's AI solution is cheaper than the Myers-Briggs Type Indicator.

The closer AI gets to humans, the more humans have to maintain a close watch. The more you automate your HR processes with AI tools, the greater the need for you to test them—their accuracy, their effectiveness, and their error rate.

Supply Chain Management and Transportation

We treat supply chain management, an essential pillar of modern industrial economies, in the same category as transportation because both move products as well as people. People, of course, are not products, but AI tools for logistics can help to move both more efficiently and effectively. A survey of senior supply chain management executives showed that 65 percent view their industry as being on the cusp of revolutionary change, for the better.[76]

Those of us who take supply chain management for granted should dwell for a second on the complex statistical relationships among warehouses, items, required storage conditions, inventories, vehicles of all kinds, drivers, and delivery personnel. We now have data on everything, all the time. Large cargo carriers have been tracked by satellite for decades, but add to that the Internet of Things and vast data processing, and the following are possible:

- Real-time optimization of carrier selection—vehicle, route, schedules, etc. The foundation is the ability to know where all people, vehicles, and items are at any given moment. Tracking data is key. Equally vital are data from delivery history, current and anticipated weather, and real-time customer feedback.
- Storage optimization. Linear Logistics, a cold food storage and delivery service, used AI analytics to help them to arrange pallets according to delivery timing. They boosted the efficiency of their pallet retrieval by 20 percent.
- Warehouse worker augmentation. Intelligrated makes voice-directed systems for guiding workers in warehouses to save time and cost. Honeywell, the great American, international conglomerate, spent $1.5 billion to acquire Intelligrated, and Honeywell's sales have soared since then.[77] It also spent $490 million on Transnorm, a German warehouse automation company.
- Route optimization. UPS uses an On-Road Integrated Optimization and Navigation (ORION) AI tool integrated with

GPS systems for this purpose. UPS claims that it has reduced its total driven miles by perhaps 100 million, saving
the company $50 million per year, to say nothing of the
environmental costs.

- Preventive maintenance of vehicles. Delivery vehicle breakdowns cause late deliveries and can disrupt the entire supply
chain. Continual analysis of data collected from all parts of
the machines, relative to environmental conditions, can recommend optimally timed maintenance. The cost of intelligent, data-based, preventive vehicle maintenance should off-
set all the costs associated with breakdowns and the delays
that everyone hates.

- Autonomous cargo ships. On the high seas, Rolls-Royce is
partnering with Intel to develop crew-less ships, bristling
with radar, LIDAR (light detection and ranging), thermal,
and HD sensors and cameras and equipped with AI processors to manage the data. They are programmed to steer away
from all forms of obstacles and threats, and they are com-
manded by a crew on land. They ought to perform better,
given that the vast majority of ship losses are due to human
error.

- Self-driving trucks work in a similar way. The US Postal
Service is piloting use of TuSimple's self-driving trucks on a
long haul with low traffic (Dallas to Phoenix).[78] The forty-
five-hour, 2,100-mile round-trip is brutal on human drivers.
The technology performs better than humans in terms of
driver error and accidents.

- Flying robo-taxis are here. At least six companies in the
United States, Germany, and China have developed battery-
powered drones that can deliver one to two passengers at
least a dozen miles with vertical liftoff and landing capability.
AI will determine the flight path and stabilize the journey.
There is no room for a human pilot in the vehicle, though
there will be human oversight located in command centers.[79]

Retail delivery logistics and, actually, the whole of the supply chain management is an enormous AI growth area. Amazon alone spent $800 million in one quarter in 2019 to keep its logistics system state-of-the-art. Massive UPS operates all across the globe, handling 19 million packages per day, conveyed by 96,000 vehicles. The pressure to route for the greatest efficiency and to deliver to the customer on time never lets up. Every day there are fluctuating factors—such as weather or roadwork or car accidents or airport disruptions—and AI takes those into account in real time, while recommending routing paths. UPS has invested in chatbots for customer service that field the usual scripted questions that we all have about our expected deliveries. And get ready for deliveries of light, highly time-sensitive packages via autonomous drone. The technology is already tested and has been deployed in select areas.[80]

And then, of course, there are the self-driving cars that everyone knows about. AI is changing the nature of the mobility industry, and many companies are vying for a piece of the action. In Silicon Valley, Uber, Tesla, and Alphabet's Waymo lead work on autonomous driving systems, and car-making companies around the world are working either in consort or in competition with these leaders.

GM, for example, took investment from SoftBank and Honda for its Cruise project. Ford poured $1 billion into its AI Argo work, is reaching out to rivals for collaboration, and plans an $11 billion restructuring to move into mass production. Ford and Walmart are putting together a self-driving service. Toyota is teaming up with Uber to deploy its self-driving technology into Toyota's vehicles, and Volvo has agreed to supply thousands of SUVs for Uber's growing autonomous fleet. One way or another, American, German, and Japanese automotive giants are gearing up to compete fiercely with Tesla and Waymo in the self-driving car market.

Another potentially enormous market opportunity will be driverless systems for "normal" cars, called "advanced driver-assistance systems" (ADAS). A successful product is an affordable, compact system that helps human drivers put on the brakes in time to avoid a collision. The idea is not to build a driverless car, but to help convert normal cars into driverless vehicles in optimal circumstances like good weather and relaxed traffic conditions. In fog, rain, or snow, however, the human should assume full control. For data, it relies on multiple digital cameras attached to the car. Radar and LIDAR can be added to the system as backups or supplements. Intel recently purchased Mobileye, an Israeli start-up, for $15 billion, makers of collision-avoidance equipment installed in more than 15 million vehicles as of 2017.[81] Intel, Mobileye, and BMW are developing autonomous vehicles, and Intel, Mobileye, and Volkswagen are working to launch a self-driving car service in Israel.

Because mobility applies to people first and large, heavy metal machines next, there are a host of services that can be offered for mobility consumers and providers when the main beneficiary does not need to watch the road. An exciting prospect for managers and workers of all kinds is adding personal productivity to the self-driving car's capacity.

Toyota wants to give car owners a more complete sync with their smartphones. Your car could warn you if you have left your phone somewhere else and not brought it with you when you return to your vehicle. While you are out of your car, it would send you a warning via your phone if your tire pressure falls below an acceptable level. If you are stuck in traffic, your car can set up a remote connection so that you don't have to miss the planned meeting. It goes without saying that a car should have an AI-powered voice-operated system that is trained to respond to you, so that your hands can be free to take care of other tasks.

AI service offerings run the gamut. Uber has even applied for a patent on an AI system to determine if the person who ordered a ride is drunk, in order to warn the prospective Uber driver appropriately. The algorithm takes into account how fast that person types, how many mistakes they make, whether they correct them, how accurate the person presses buttons in the Uber app, how fast they have been walking, how the phone is held (or even dropped), and which establishments, such as bars, they have been in, and for how long.[82] For ride-sharing, of course, security is a prime consideration, for the driver as much as for the rider.

Autonomous transportation is taking off, literally, above and beyond automobiles. China's DeepBlue sells its "smart Panda bus" to cities in China, Thailand, and Greece. Flying cars and bikes are already here. Police in Dubai plan to introduce electric hoverbikes in 2020, even if they can fly with their pilot for only ten to twenty-five minutes on battery power. Uber's flying vehicle project, Uber Elevate, can convey people for short jaunts over traffic jams in crowded cities. Without AI self-optimizing algorithms, such a human transportation system would be unthinkable.

Education

Education is immensely tough for machines because it is a supremely human activity. People learn in their own way. Some are more visual learners; others learn better through listening, while others need to take in the whole experience and participate actively. Then there is a host of distractions, pressures, learning disabilities, and various hindrances. And people learn some subjects better than others. Individual learning aptitudes and styles render a machine-like approach to education dubious at best.

Current schooling systems put students on a conveyor belt toward equal outcomes. Teachers are supposed to teach uniform material and help along the slower learners, and the result is that the system effectively slows down quicker learners. In the history of education, the development of this industrial approach runs roughly parallel to the rise of mass production and assembly lines in the late-nineteenth and early-twentieth centuries. We don't imply that education was better before then, even if its greater reliance on individual tutors made it more personal. Can it be that interactive, AI-powered learning assistance software will allow education to revert to a more self-paced, individuated learning on a large scale?

Swedish start-up Sana Labs aims to do exactly that. Partnering with large-scale academic publishers and online learning platforms, Sana Labs's AI aims to predict a student's future errors—say, in math or a foreign language—based on past and real-time performance data. The learning management system could then prompt the student to exercise that particular weakness in a number of ways until knowledge acquisition is demonstrably complete. Sana Labs's error-prediction algorithms won in Duo Lingo's Global AI competition in English, Spanish, and French.[83]

In addition to assisting learners, AI software can also help teachers with the more-onerous, repetitive tasks, such as grading. China, with its millennia-old preference for standardized tests, is leading the way in the effort to automate grading. Apparently one-quarter of all Chinese schools (about 60,000, involving 120 million young people) are supplying data sets of student essays for trained AI grading algorithms that should indicate areas of improvement in structure and style. Participating Chinese schools, however, gave the system a bad grade because there were too many instances where a superb essay was scored poorly.[84] Writing is not reckoning. Language is not math. Computers are wonderful for mathematical calculations. They cannot replicate the ultimately mysterious processes of language-based human thought.

Another need for AI is in school safety, especially given the appalling rate of abuse and shootings in the United States. Some districts have hired software firms to monitor and analyze student use of school laptops and tablets in order to make predictions about potentially harmful behavior, whether directed toward one-self or others. Gaggle, in addition to offering software that combs school learning systems for noxious, harmful content, also includes a safety tip line called "SpeakUp," where students can report bullying, fights, and all threats of violence within the school, in real time.[85] Securly, used by ten thousand schools with 10 million young students, offers functions similar to Gaggle's, but it can cover students' personal devices and social media activity as well.[86] AI monitoring is a new and effective tool for school teachers and staff to obtain early warnings and aid students in need of better security.

Education, in schools and on the job, is the best tool to prepare people for successful AI implementation.[87] AI can help both teachers and learners. Concern that machines will render teachers obsolete are wildly exaggerated. There is much more to teaching the young than the transfer of data, information, and argument. The human element cannot be replaced by hardware and software.

Education in AI can also help make it available to everyone. There have been many complaints that AI is white and male through and through. Facial recognition software is demonstrably less effective on people with darker skin. Amazon's infamous HR hiring algorithm excluded women in preference of men. Latin and African Americans are sorely lacking in AI companies. But there are signs that the tide is slowly turning. The first free English–Spanish dictionary of AI terms is available on GitHub.[88] AI courses and education materials are available online for free to anyone keen to learn.

Agriculture

There are many exciting developments in this ancient occupation that reduce waste, chemical pollution, disease, and drudgery. For nearly two centuries, mechanization and automation have achieved extraordinary gains in agricultural productivity. AI is pushing the next wave, and it will make farming more efficient, cleaner, and healthier. Many parts of sub-Saharan Africa have leapfrogged landline telephones for smartphones. It is a matter of time till AI increases efficiencies for poor farmers across the globe.

Below are some AI applications in the field of agriculture:

- Connecterra sells a "Fitbit" for cows and powers its diagnostics on Google's TensorFlow.[89] Real-time data about the animal's basic symptoms are used to deploy veterinarians early on, before the animal gets seriously ill. Healthy livestock means healthier meat and dairy products.

- Use of trained AI image recognition that determines the right amount of fertilizer for lettuces and other plants, based on their size and development. We may very well see a significant shift away from spraying whole fields to treating individual plants with what they need, and no more.

- Swiss company ecoRobotix, Blue River in Silicon Valley, and other firms sell robots that trundle across cultivated fields, take pictures of every plant, and either pluck or spray those classified as weeds. Some machines use herbicide, and other use concentrated fertilizer, which can also kill young weeds. This machine raises hopes that the day of spraying whole fields with herbicides indiscriminately are numbered.

- Image recognition software is even being applied to fish faces. IFarm has produced a scanner that differentiates farmed salmon by the individual markings on their heads. Industrial-sized fish farmers use it to help sort out the fish that show signs of infectious disease and remove them from the pond or batch.

- Agri-giant Cargill Inc. is using a similar technology from an Irish AI start-up to learn cattle faces and track each animal's food and water consumption. If they spot the ones that quit eating and drinking, then they stand a better chance of stopping disease from spreading through the herd.

- Taranis specializes in processing of high-resolution photos and video taken from powerful sensors on aircraft that can cover 50,000 acres per day.[90] The images are clear enough for a trained AI algorithm to count the number of beetles and categorize discoloring visible on leaf tops. Taranis counts crops, measures growth, registers weed intrusions, and predicts yields. Processed reports are sent to smartphones and tablets. Farmers take time saved on diagnostics and apply it to solving the problems. Taranis is already working on 19,000 farms across the world.

- Iron Ox and Bowery Farming have raised millions of dollars to implement fully automated, organic, indoor farms. Plenty raised $200 million from SoftBank to develop vertical farms of ultra-organic produce, not including trees and root vegetables, obviously. Aerofarms, BrightFarms, and Freight Farms are also working on indoor, completely pesticide-free farming. AI systems monitor growth and health.

Of course, all agricultural AI machines that perform the hard work of attending to individual plants and animals will have to deal with dust, bad weather, and rough ground or water conditions that hamper performance and require constant servicing. These are real occupational hazards, but we would all prefer that machines relieve the humans of the worst of the drudgery and the exposure to chemicals.

Surveillance and Security

We live in a world of ubiquitous digital eyes and constant data collection. Cameras are installed at ever more doors and hallways. Drones of all sizes fly about, gather images and other data, and relay it for analysis. Both a blessing and a curse, surveillance technology can enhance security even as it degrades privacy.

AI-powered image tagging offers many applications to enhance safety for organizations. Again, the strength of such solutions lies in their ability to enhance the range and accuracy of human oversight. When it comes to security, we recommend embracing the cyborg.

Facial identification can supplement other protections at secure points of entry and exit in just about any building you can think of, or any computer device with a camera. It's in place at many major airports throughout the world, and miscreants have been caught trying to enter countries with a stolen or falsified ID. It's in laptops, smartphones, tablets, and so on, to spare users the hassle of repeated password entries. Banks and stores use it in China for ATM functions and as a payment mechanism.

Video "recognition" works pretty much the same as with images. A video is, after all, more or less just a series of pictures. Sigma AI analyzes security camera video to detect suspicious and hostile movements, such as human figures moving into restricted areas or lingering in places where most people merely pass through.[91] Sigma software surveys items and tags anything that might be a weapon, concealed or unconcealed.

Eyesight Technologies, an Israeli start-up, markets an in-car device that scans and analyzes the driver's face for signs of distraction, weariness, or drug use according to head position, facial direction, eye direction, blinks per minute, and pupil dilation.[92] Eyesight's DriverSense integrates with the car's sound system, so it has a number of ways to get the driver's attention or wake them up. Affectiva has a similar solution that monitors drivers and passengers in traditional and self-driving automobiles, looking for signs of distraction and distress, including children left in the backseat. The goal is to mitigate misbehavior, one could say, before it causes a traffic accident.[93]

Athena Security works to tag school shooters caught on video before they open fire.[94] To mitigate this appalling problem in the United States, Athena's system alerts school administration and local police as soon as it tags an image of any kind of gun on school property. Should any shooting begin, Athena broadcasts loud announcements throughout school buildings that the authorities are on the way, which has been shown to deter or slow down at least some mass murderers. Athena can work as a stand-alone solution or with already-installed security camera systems, and, yet again, is meant to supplement human monitors proactively, not replace them.

Drones are a category unto themselves, but they are basically floating, flying sensor platforms with some capability for very light delivery. Many people use them for fun, filming themselves from aloft, and spying on the neighborhood. Others use them to make sure that they and their close interactions with others are watched and recorded, presumably to deter harassment, stalkers, burglars, and others.

You should be aware, however, of the unsettling claim that drones made in China send a copy of all data recorded back to Beijing.[95] Better think twice about where you fly them. You may not care if Chinese authorities have recordings of your backyard, but video of airports, power plants, and military installations should give everyone pause.

Fleets of drones backed up by AI image tagging can greatly assist teams of people searching for missing persons, especially in unsettled, wilderness areas. Farmers can use drones and analysis of their data for rapid surveying of fields and livestock to raise awareness of agricultural problems and prioritize addressing them.

Zipline specializes in drones for aerial delivery. It started in Rwanda, delivering blood upon demand to clinics and medical centers in the inaccessible mountain areas and remote savannahs.[96] Recently Zipline has been working with Amazon to perform aerial deliveries in the UK. In addition to their current pilot project in Australia, they have been getting ready to work in the United States, pending authorization from federal and state governments. Amazon and FedEx are rolling out drone delivery of consumer products in 2020.

Drone flight patterns can be optimized based on historical performance under a multitude of conditions, from wind and dust to direct attack. These machine learning algorithms are similar to those at work in self-driving cars and trucks. Shield AI makes mini drones that fly into buildings to map out their interiors, including occupant whereabouts, which can be used primarily to increase intelligence and reduce casualties in hostage situations and areas of military conflict.[97] Shield is working to train drones to respond to all kinds of unfavorable flying conditions.

NASA is developing a "national traffic management system" for US cities and rural areas, for drones operated individually and those that run on autonomous aerial guidance systems. Drones need to be restricted from risky and sensitive areas. They need to be tracked and identified, but human air traffic controllers will never be able to keep track of them all. The system has to be fundamentally different from the one for airplanes and airlines. With AI, it's practically unthinkable, but humans will have to be kept in the loop at all times.[98]

In addition to physical security is the world of the nonphysical: cybersecurity. When it comes to protecting your systems, your data, and your intellectual property, human oversight is simply inadequate, and too costly. AI algorithms can tag anomalous data flows, such as when a certain coworker's laptop suddenly starts transferring terabytes of data to some unknown IP address. Cybersecurity companies that use AI usually rely on data derived from a firm's firewall, but that is little help against spyware preinstalled on hardware elements.

Again, beware of overblown marketing. Darktrace's marketing team likes to compare its cloud-based AI cybersecurity solution to the human body's immune system.[99] The firm even named its chief AI product "Antigena," which stops ransomware, malware, and other threats. The immune system metaphor resonates with every human customer, but it distorts how the software actually works in customers' networks, servers, computer environments, and control systems. AI algorithms have almost nothing in common with white blood cells.

Digital content is in desperate need of cleaning and protection, and image "recognition" can help. Start-up Clarifai says its algorithms can apply filters for images that are "explicit," "suggestive," "not safe for work," etc.[100] Microsoft Azure's Content Moderator claims to be able to winnow out offensive pictures, words, phrases, and video content, of many ilks. But of course you should never rely exclusively on such AI applications. If identifying a simple cat was such a huge challenge, imagine the difficulty of classifying arrays of pixels as "suggestive." "I know it when I see it," is a human response to the problem of technically defining obscenity.[101]

Facebook's answer to its horrible problem of people posting inappropriate content has been to use filtering algorithms but also pay for "content moderators," more than 15,000 in 2019, up from 7,500 in 2018, and 4,500 in 2017. The problem can be helped by AI technology, but not solved. We people can't code decency any more than we can legislate it.

Cybersecurity grows more important by the day. The more organizations use AI for task automation and worker augmentation, the more essential those systems become for daily operations, and the greater the existential risk if a hacker savages your code— or swipes it. From anywhere in the world, adversarial governments, terrorists, criminals, and kids looking for fun pose a risk to cyber systems.

Whatever you do with AI, make sure that you have the cybersecurity to match it!

Military AI

AI-powered weaponry is already here, and there is no use protesting it. At the time of writing, the Pentagon is running six hundred different programs that use AI in various military activities.[102] The vast majority of those programs involve business functions—payroll and back office, equipment maintenance, paralegal work, natural language processing, virtual helpdesk chatbots, etc.—and less than fifty concern weapons, defensive and offensive.

The fact is that semi- to fully autonomous weapons are the present and the future. Silicon Valley libertarians may dream of a world where technology renders military structures, personnel, and activities obsolete, but for that you would need a new kind of human being. On Earth we are heading toward 8 billion of one kind. We are not equipped for Utopia. Let those who think themselves above the rest of us give it a go on Mars.

For a couple of centuries now, people have fought primarily with mechanisms, principally guns and explosives, rather than with simpler items such as blades, stone, or sticks. Drones and robots merely increase our ability to deliver the effect of those mechanisms while reducing the immediate risk to our soldiers. Self-driving, self-aiming armored transports with machine guns and antitank missiles, autonomous tanks, and flying guns dispatched to take out enemy forces are already here. Everyone wants their own troops out of harm's way. Many want to reduce "collateral damage." AI can help. AI facial, image, and video recognition, combined with mobility machine learning and constant predictive analytics, is the logical present and future of US counterterrorism operations and military combat.

Was there ever a time in human history when new technologies were not applied to armed conflict? Yes. Opposing sides in World War II did not use chemical weapons, although they had them. Moral repugnance had something to do with it, but fear of retaliation in kind was probably more compelling. Furthermore, gases and nerve agents were tactically unwieldy, floating wherever the winds took them. Using them in the past may have brought passing tactical success, but never a strategic victory.

The US military raised its spending on AI from $1.44 billion in fiscal 2017 to $1.88 billion in fiscal 2019. The sheer volume of data gathered by the military and its commercial supporters, from all the satellites, drones, and everything else, cries out for the most-advanced analytic tools. Robots that defuse bombs and clear minefields are desperately needed. For men and women in combat, good situational awareness at critical moments is paramount.

The Air Force's Project Maven has led the way with its object detection and classification algorithms applied to digitized images and video. The goal is to equip soldiers with computer-enhanced vision capability that helps them with orientation, mission objectives, and threat identification. Spokespersons routinely deny that the technology will actually select targets, but it is certainly meant to help people do so. Young, tired, stressed, and scared soldiers in the crucible of combat need the best tools available to assist with legitimate targeting. The fewer civilian deaths, the better. Of course, the performance and accuracy of the system is reliant on training data sets and high-quality data, just like every other AI system.

An uproar among Google's employees led the firm to end its work on Project Maven by 2019, and to draft ethical standards for future military work. While we laud Google's interest in ethics and law, it needs to be less selective and occasional. A worrisome example is Google's work for China's single-party, surveillance state.

A whistleblower revealed that Google was working to develop a censored search engine, called Project Dragonfly, for the Chinese government, one that links users' phone numbers to their record of search terms, publishes only government-sanctioned information about air quality, and cannot search for "human rights," "student protest," "Nobel prize," and many phrases that include "Xi Jinping."[103] Others claimed that it granted the Chinese government access to all parts of a user's computer. What Google does—tracking users on the web—supports more than one authoritarian regime with an appalling record on human rights. Bad press presumably led Google to end work on Project Dragonfly, which was announced in a grilling interrogation in the US Congress in July 2019.

Googlers protest their company's collusion with the US government, so others step into the gap. Radiant Solutions (a division of Maxar Technologies) is a booming AI business in Virginia, profiting from a surging flow of contracts from the US Department of Defense.[104] The goal is to enhance military intelligence through massive data collection from satellites, drones, and other airborne vehicles that use optical and radar technologies, and to automate analysis of all that image and video content.

The United States has a long, historical tradition of collaboration between government and the private sector for defensive and offensive purposes. The incentives for private companies to participate are too significant for all but the very richest to ignore. Among rival powers, such as Russia and China, libertarian qualms and shows of resistance carry no weight, and can incur hefty penalties.

On a more prosaic level, the US military, with its vast arsenal of machines, has millions and millions of parts to monitor, maintain, and replace as they wear out. Uptake Technologies specializes in

AI-powered predictions as to when vehicles will no longer operate.[105] Sensors in the machines gather data about temperature,
coolant levels, transmission stress, etc., and Uptake provides the
feedback. Not confined to the military, Uptake software surveys
Boeings, Caterpillars, and wind turbines.[106]

We could have added sections for retail and wholesale business
operations, for energy production and distribution, for the sports
entertainment industry, for government and the legal world, but
you have the idea: AI's five main functions listed at the beginning
of the chapter have more uses and applications for people working
than anyone can think of.

This section has been about other organizations. The rest of the
book is about yours: how you need to manage your data, implement your AI, guarantee that it makes you money, and how to
govern your system so that it does not run you into a wall.

4

AI SUCCESS IN YOUR ORGANIZATION

Now you have learned what AI is, how it works, what it can do, what it can't, and how entrepreneurs are deploying it across the whole economy. You're probably thinking, "How do I start? What do I do at my company to benefit from AI tech?"

The sobering pattern is that up to one-half of all AI projects fail. Based on responses from 2,473 organizations that are now using AI, a clear majority reported failed implementations, and around 600 admitted to a 50 percent failure rate.[1] This chapter is about how *not* to join that club.

In order to achieve success, let's start with the point of it all.

KEEP IT SIMPLE: MAKE MONEY

At this point, let's drop the family metaphor for AI, where mom is data, dad is math, and AI systems are little, individual kids. Having children, adopting children, is a self-giving act. AI is a set of tools, not an individual human being.

You should only adopt AI into your organization if it makes money. Let's be clear and direct: The point of a firm is to make money. If the firm loses money, it is going to die, eventually, and the work will be in vain. So firms need to make money. Only adopt an AI solution if the path to profit is well-planned and clear.

Nonprofits can be a little different, of course, but not completely. They need to make money, too, to carry out operations and cover their costs. They have no pressure to distribute earnings to shareholders, but if they lose money in their normal operations, then they need donations to cover the shortfall. If they don't, they lose money; they will have trouble doing what they set out to do, and they will die. The work will be in vain. A nonprofit should only adopt an AI solution if it is going to help it make money or spend less money.

Governments, on the other hand, can always tax, so they won't die. Government entities have to serve their constituents, at least to some extent, in order to justify their funding. Given the normal limitations of budgets, they frequently face cost pressures. Many government entities are working to do more with less. A government agency or department should only adopt an AI solution if it can result in cost savings or higher performance of services.

Managers of for-profits, nonprofits, and government entities should have costs and performance in mind. The way to higher profit and better performance is to enhance the productivity and effectiveness of your people. AI is a tool set that can augment people's labor. Never implement AI for its own sake, just because someone else has it, or it seems cutting-edge, or what have you.

For your first AI project, start with something simple, and keep it simple. It has to make you money or save you money. And your first project has to be a win, even though the odds are not really in your favor. To avoid the same failure that occurs in half of all AI implementations, Hilary Mason, founder and CEO of Fast Forward Labs and data scientist in residence at VC firm Accel Partners, advises, "we need to make [AI] about results and outcomes and about using the simple-as-possible approach that will suffice to get you those results and outcomes. If it happens to be mathematically cool, boy will I be happy, but that's really not the point."[2]

And give it time. Successful AI adoption takes much longer than your average out-of-the-box software installation. Dongyan

Wang, VP of AI transformation at Landing.AI, a company founded by Andrew Ng that specializes in AI implementation, said, "It takes about eighteen to twenty-four months to understand [the] clients' needs and help them develop an internal AI team and strategy."[3] That is for major projects. Give no less than six to nine months for the first small AI project that you tackle. Don't risk an early loss when you can insure a well-defined win. Follow well-established business best practices. Plan it. Organize it. Lead it. Control it.

Let's tackle the plan phase first: Plan AI adoption like an accountant, and a real leader.

PLAN like an Accountant and a Leader

In the plan phase, let's start with your accountant role. Always bear in mind the basic accounting formula for firms:

Revenues (money people pay you for goods and services)
Minus Cost of Goods Sold (money you pay to provide those goods and services)
Minus Expenses (money you pay for sales and administrative overhead)
Equals Net Profit.

This little equation can and should apply to every kind of human organization that uses money. Your organization works to do or make something for people, to provide some kind of good or service. It costs your organization a certain amount of money to do that work. And then there are expenses that you must pay for your organization to exist and operate, such as rent, leases, compliance and legal fees, taxes (maybe), payroll, accounting, document management, IT, phones, office software, security, PR, outreach, and the sales team. Profit is left over.

Take a close look at where the firm spends its money. Identify and list all areas of the business that do not generate any revenue. They are normally in the areas of HR and administration, but there can be many areas of questionable value and outright waste in sales and operations. Conduct your financial probing with your internal accountants and lead financial people. Look to increase the efficiency of your overhead so that you get more for your money, and to increase the effectiveness of your sales team so that you get more business.

Your goal is to match the money you spend on AI implementation to money you save in areas where you are spending it with limited to no return. Overhead is essential for every business, but because it generates no revenue, the work needs to be done as efficiently as possible.

On the revenue side, your goal is to invest in an AI tool that increases your total sales significantly beyond the AI implementation expense. Match your enhanced data analytics and automation tools to the higher sales they actually bring in. The goal is not to automate sales and get rid of the team—that would be crazy—but to make them more effective in their work. You have to budget and control your investment in AI in terms of money spent and people's time invested.

Make sure that you define in quantitative terms what success looks like. This is an essential step. How much money is it reasonable for you to save from the investment in AI? How much more revenue can you reasonably expect to bring in because of it? You need to set financial goals in order to know whether the project succeeded or failed, and by how much.

As you set your goals, forget the pies in the sky. Be sober and skeptical. Remember MD Anderson's squandered $62 million that went to IBM and PricewaterhouseCoopers in an attempt to "take on cancer," whatever that means. And GE Digital spent $7 billion on three thousand programmers building an AI system to unify their hundreds of enterprise applications into a functional, intelligent whole. The division fell apart, and the CEO went on to lose his job.[4] They might as well have gone to Mars. If you are using an AI vendor, take the salesperson's predictions with a big pinch of salt. They don't know your business the way you do.

So, if the numbers don't add up, bag it. No tool is worth using if it doesn't save you and your people money, time, and effort, or result in more—and better—business. Conduct the financial analysis of your firm as coolly and rationally as possible. The only thing that matters in this particular exercise is the facts. Completely insulate yourself from histrionic marketing of AI software services. The AI business landscape is pocked with hyperbole.

And there's no need to keep this financial accounting work quiet or hidden at your organization. Such analysis is a good business practice. And you will balance it with good, human leadership.

At the same time as you conduct your financial analysis of the firm, plan a major movement within the firm, a cultural shift, toward AI. If you have planned and led these before, then it's time for another one. If you have never done one before, one is overdue. Embrace the opportunity, and don't fear it.

Plan AI adoption as a team effort. Produce and communicate positive energy and interest in AI for your business entity, because it is a big deal, and needs a lot of personal buy-in, education, and transformation in order to secure success.

Above all, let your employees know that you want to listen, that you are listening, and that you will listen to them the whole way. Encourage them to be daring about rethinking the way they and everyone else works. Open live and online discussion forums. Set up venues to gather and record ideas. Let your employees know that AI adoption and implementation benefits from everyone's input. If you cannot lead this effort, appoint someone else who can.

Invest in basic education about AI. The educational resources are available online for free. Either give your people time off to learn about AI or pay them for their time and effort. Work that line item into the budget. Teach them from this book about AI's actual, functional capabilities. Cite examples of AI applications across various industries. If you have an advisory board, you will need to engage them in productive dialogue and secure their support as well.[5]

But *listen* above all! What are the business problems that people want to solve? What do people think can be learned from the organization's data? Find out the tasks that people perform that are dull, repetitive, and nearly brainless. Make an inventory of those tasks. At the same time, ask people the number-one problems that they face in their jobs, the problems they would like more time to work on and solve, the problems they could be working on if they didn't have to spend so much time on dull, repetitive, nearly brainless activities. Communicate positively. Let people know that the goal is to empower them and augment their work, not to replace them with a dumb machine.

The accountant and the leader. Wear both hats as you plan. The accountant in you will work to see cost savings and higher revenue in your bottom line. The leader in you will work in tandem with your people to create a new organizational culture supporting AI innovation.

Here are the planning tasks in brief:

- Conduct financial analysis of the institution.
- Initiate a cultural shift and AI education.
- Gather suggestions for AI implementation.
- Prioritize them based on benefits and costs.

As we said before, clearly define what success looks like. Set targets so that you can measure progress as you proceed.

ORGANIZE According to Plan

The planning phase will have revealed your top people in the AI adoption process, those who can and want to learn, those with the best implementation ideas, those who can reimagine the work of your business at the 10,000-foot level, and can also make things happen on the ground. Organize these people into implementation teams.

Have a special team to articulate your AI ethics and legal compliance. Obtain outside legal counsel where you need assistance.

Flatten your management structure of the projects and widen the span.

Determine the optimal balance of distributed vs. centralized authority over the projects, relative to the structure of your entity, in order to maximize communication and coordination among the teams. The bigger you are, of course, the harder it gets, especially if you are conglomerate, multidivisional, or matrix in form.

In the *Plan* phase, you initiated the culture shift. In the *Organize* phase, you make sure that you communicate to your people the need for AI adoption. Articulate clear goals for each project. Show everyone what success looks like.

Based on the cost–benefit analysis, set clear, rational budgets for each project.

Obtain and allocate funding, including employee rewards systems.

Consolidate your data. This can be a major project in and of itself. Develop a full and complete inventory. Where is your data right now? What state is its quality? What is its state of completeness? How ready is your data for AI analysis and adoption? If feasible, resettle your data into one coherent, logical, accessible database warehouse. Depending on your need for privacy, security, and convenience, build your database in hardware "on prem" (on your organization's physical premises) or in the cloud. The last thing you want is to have internal data silos hamper the performance of any AI system you develop.

Finally, in the *Organize* phase, determine whether to adopt a full in-house, hybrid-hosted, or full outsourced approach. These apply to people and tech together.

If you have the in-house talent and hardware, go for it on your first, well-defined, simple project. Have your people acquire the necessary coding knowledge of AI machine learning algorithms through the free courses and training programs on educational sites such as Coursera.org. Learn directly from the best. Andrew Ng shares his knowledge with everyone for free, no strings attached. In the full in-house scenario, you keep your data in hardware on premise and conduct all your AI data analytics there as well. You do not use outside vendor or cloud-based platforms.

In the hybrid-hosted approach, you and your team select your first projects, taking full ownership of the management processes, but you rely on outside vendors to provide specific AI tools to accomplish your task. You consolidate and prepare your data for AI analytics, but you transfer it to the databases of a cloud-based AI provider. You hire consultant data scientists to perform the technical AI implementation work that you and your team lack the expertise to perform. A certain risk lies in depending on outsiders, but the advantage is that your organization supplements your current capabilities to augment your work in new ways. Your organization will benefit from the success and gain from the know-how. The cost will be limited to the project parameters.

In the full outsourced implementation, you hire an outside team of AI professionals to conduct and complete the implementation project for you. No need for you to hire full-time data scientists or AI developers into your firm's ranks. Your AI vendor will come with a team, examine your data and your processes, pitch various projects for you to choose from, and will take care of all stages of project design and execution. The risk lies in their consulting more with their own people than with yours. They might develop and install a template solution that fits their needs better than yours. Another risk lies in the aftermath, when all is said and done, and they pack up and go. Governance and maintenance of the system lies with you. You need someone committed to your team who will keep tabs, test, and verify proper performance.

Of vital importance in both the hosted-hybrid and full outsourced approaches is the selection of AI platforms and vendors. Choose the one with a realistic sales pitch, and focus on data, ethics, and legal compliance, as well as on the actual chance of success, relative to the cost.

You know, the first project can be as simple as developing a little chatbot. No need to dive into machine learning algorithms from the get-go if you and your team are not ready. For example, a coworker who handles PR and community outreach complains that 95 percent of the calls she receives ask for the same five items of basic information. She would much rather spend her time on developing a new program that aims to tap into a whole new line of business. She wants to use her PR work for direct, measurable business development rather than repeating the same five pieces of information throughout the day.

She can build her own chatbot to take care of it, for cheap.

Use Dexter. Go to https://rundexter.com, open an account, and read the documentation instructions.[6] The site allows you to build your own simple chatbot. You take care of the words, and the site takes care of the code. You can then embed that code in an HTML website if you like. You can install your bot in Facebook Messenger or integrate it with Google's TensorFlow for natural language processing if you want to upgrade its capabilities. You can also run your bot using SMS telephone technology if you pair it up with a telephony service vendor such as Twilio. You can run your bot on Amazon's Alexa with voiced prompts. Try it for free for fourteen days and see what your people can do with it in that time frame.

No, this is not an example of self-optimizing AI algorithms that use backpropagation, but it is a clear step that empowers an employee to augment her work by automating a dull, repetitive task that has hindered her from adding more value or solving a real problem.

Start small, but you can also aim for bigger game.

For your customer service needs, for example, you can design and implement a virtual assistant, with a name, simple persona, and a list of tasks that it can complete, a set that can grow over time. The key measure of success for each automated task implementation is customer satisfaction and delight in their experience with the virtual assistant. You can start with an online chatbot, then add voice commands when you are ready.

Telefónica, a world-class telecom company with nearly $50 billion a year in revenue, developed and rolled out Aura, an AI system that uses company data about their customers to serve their customers, the way the customer wants. Aura enables the customer to talk to the system to get tasks completed in real time. Aura also gives customers full control of their data, with full transparency on how that data is used. Telefónica started this project in 2010 and is still working to improve it.[7]

LEAD like a General, and a Servant

Yep, I mean it. Lead your people like an excellent military leader. Engage, exhort, and inspire them. It's about the unified effort, not you. The moment you stop listening, you start the solo show, and you are on the road to self-centered, deaf management, wasted effort, and failure. Serve the effort, not yourself.

Marshal your resources. Don't waste time and money. Steward your organization's resources meticulously, and that includes people's valuable time. Start meetings and finish them on time. Let your mantra be, "No agenda, no meeting." Punctuality is simply professional. Working mindfully with respect to time does not mean that you hurry or give into the pressure to rush. If a major problem emerges for the meeting agenda, allot ample time to solve it. Consider using the daily scrum: a meeting where all participants provide brief, tight updates and leave with a clear, manageable to-do list. People come prepared, work together, and wind up knowing what they are doing next.

Make sure milestones and deadlines are met. Make sure things happen the way the team planned them. You know what success looks like. Serve your teams' efforts so that they achieve success. Don't even think of micromanaging. Schedule regular check-in meetings with key team leaders to assess progress. Delegate wherever possible, and hold people to account.

Now let's face facts: You will encounter resistance, and you will have to fire employees. Resistance from people is inevitable in the face of every change, and there will be plenty who cross their arms and dig in their heels when they hear terms like *artificial intelligence*. People will resist out of uncertainty, fear, or lack of comprehension, or because of a problem at home, or because they just prefer to go on working at their present level of inefficiency. Poor performers routinely resist movements toward higher achievement. Others will really, honestly believe that what you are doing is bad for the company. They feel that they, and everyone else, will lose. Take resistance as a given. You will have to contend with it.

Wherever you can, co-opt resistance. Take initial objections, concerns, and warnings as signs of engagement rather than obstinacy. Give people time and opportunity to change their negative attitudes. Invite critical minds to learn more about AI tech, to investigate more deeply how it could augment coworkers' work, and to join the AI implementation teams in order to guarantee success. Communicate constantly. Show and celebrate success whenever and wherever it occurs. Be positive, and don't issue blanket threats, because it looks hollow, petty, and vindictive. Those who won't take a step toward you should be ignored or sidelined. Those who learn, investigate, join, and then proceed to undermine team efforts need to leave.

A leader needs to identify and eliminate losses. In a manner of speaking, a leader also needs to be a healer, and healing takes action, timing, and patience. Sometimes the healer has to stop hemorrhages and cut out growths and tumors. Uncontrolled bleeding needs to be halted immediately, but surgery can normally wait. A surgeon in a hurry is a scary prospect for most patients. Only in rare circumstances do you need to wield the scalpel with speed.

People who perform tasks that can be reliably automated by AI and are either unwilling or unable to apply their minds and their talents to solving other business problems will need to be let go. People who hinder your process of AI adoption, whether openly and actively or with disguised subterfuge, are not players that you want on your team.

To welcome suggestions and criticism while looking out for saboteurs takes confidence and careful consideration. A good general needs lots of both.

CONTROL in Order to Know

Many people don't like the *Control* function because they think it's boring, inglorious, petty, or just a plain nuisance. They are dead wrong. Control is as vital as the planning, organization, and leadership. How else do you know how well you are doing?

In control, you only believe the facts, not the rhetoric. You keep tabs on progress according to the planned benchmarks. Each step of the way, ask yourself: "Did we meet, exceed, or fail to achieve the expected outcome?"

Here are suggested steps in the AI adoption process with the necessary controls in measurable, quantitative terms, which include the simple yes/no.

Initiate Organization Movement toward AI

- Did you conduct the financial analysis of your organization to determine where you can cut costs or increase revenue through AI automation?
- What is the total targeted sum?
- What is your total budget to implement your first AI system?
- How many listening sessions or brainstorming events did you hold for your people?
- Did you incentivize participation and achievement throughout your organization?
- How many task forces have you set up for AI implementation?

Identify Potential Deployments of Automated AI Tools

- How many entries did you assemble in a master task inventory of all the simple, repetitive tasks in administration, sales and marketing, and operations, those identified by your people as primary candidates for automated AI tools?
- Did you verify that these tasks can be automated via supervised machine learning (as defined in chapter 2) according to the five main AI functions (summed up in chapter 3)?

- Are you keeping the focus in each case on the customer, the end user, or beneficiary of your goods and services?
- Have you matched the AI tools and projects to the targeted cost savings or expected higher revenues?
- For each project, did you decide on a full in-house, hosted-hybrid, or fully outsourced solution?

Master Your Data

- Did you complete an assessment of your data, organized by kind (structured or unstructured), and rated in terms of completeness, quality, and reliability?
- Have you smashed your silos, consolidated your data, and built an accessible platform?
- Do you have a precise record about who can access your consolidated data, and procedures in place to guarantee its security?

Look under the Hood

- Have you had a software expert look into the source code of your vendor's AI solution and evaluated the algorithms to guarantee that it is really AI and not vaporware?
- Are there built-in security measures, and do you have documented business procedures to monitor and maintain them?

Govern Your AI

- Have you articulated your AI ethics code regarding security, fairness, transparency, individual rights, privacy, and accountability?
- Have you produced a list of laws that you will use to test your system for compliance?
- Have you drawn up a plan for iterative testing as conditions and data inevitably change?
- Have you established full transparency in your system for all of your stakeholders?

- Have you given your customers options about how their data is used?
- How confident are you that the system treats everyone legally and fairly?

Every organization is different, and no one knows it better than its own people, collectively. Yes, outsiders can bring in valuable insights, but they often never get to know the relevant nitty-gritty.

Above all, take the opportunity that AI presents to *rethink how your organization has designed its work*. Looks for ways to enhance people's power to solve problems, to think creatively, to innovate, strategize, and manage effectively. Use AI tools to increase knowledge and data analysis in your workforce. Use AI tools to automate tasks that can be automated, to the extent that the efficiency and effectiveness are not compromised, so that people can focus their energy on those tasks that humans do best.

Embrace the cyborg. Govern your system. Comply with the law.

5

AI GOVERNANCE
AND DATA CONTROLS

THE AI "EVENT HORIZON"

It's time.

It's Joshua, and I'm at a bar called "The Interval." The building is situated at the edge of the San Francisco Bay inside a repurposed naval base, Fort Mason, right by the docks. It's the edge of the city, and the edge of summer, 2019, heading into fall. If you walk, west by northwest, for about forty minutes, you will hit the southern foot of the Golden Gate Bridge.

To be clear—although I am technically a few dozen miles north of Silicon Valley, Stanford, etc., Fort Mason is just about ground zero for nerds in America. Well, let me correct that. Fort Mason / SF / the Bay Area is really ground zero for the nerds of the *world*. The bar comprises the first floor of an organization called the Long Now Foundation.[1]

The premise of the Long Now Foundation is that humans are too shortsighted. We are focused on fast food and fast times and not what happens in the next millennium. We are not focused on "being good ancestors." Long Now supports projects of around the ten-thousand-year range. They want to help humanity think longer term. So, what do they do, exactly?

For one project, they are building a clock that is intended to work for ten thousand years. The parts are manufactured around here, and Seattle, but it is being built inside a mountain in western Texas. Once complete, the clock in the mountain should be roughly two hundred feet tall, use no electricity whatsoever, and require minimal maintenance.

It is being built on land owned by Jeff Bezos, founder and CEO of Amazon . . . more AI connections. Perhaps the "hyper-speed evolution" of modern technology business causes a visceral allergic reaction, and a need to escape into a slower, mechanically geared time. In addition to minimizing rust, the desert is also a good escape from frenetic nerdery, even, and perhaps especially, for the nerds.

The foundation is also building a special kind of library. The volumes of the library are specially selected to help humanity rebuild itself after a major calamity. What books, you might ask, would humanity need in order to rebuild itself after an apocalypse, whether nuclear, asteroid, or AI-induced?

In fact, *The Terminator* scenario, an "AI Apocalypse," is a favorite pick among catastrophe-mongers and preppers alike. People love that flavor of doom. "Delicious!" say moviegoers all over the known world, past and present. Why does "AI Apocalypse" market so well? Why does it sound so tasty with popcorn . . . even over alien invasion, nuclear Armageddon, plague, and alternative cinematic condiments? *The Terminator* seems to strike a personal chord of fear. Machines that look just like us (but more Austrian and pumped up)! That work faster than us! Coming to kill us! Even scarier: *Coming to take our jobs!*

Maybe one should put *this* book in her or his postapocalyptic library. The rest of them—snugged upon shelves along the upper walls of the bar—are about medicine, woodcraft, computers, etc. Maybe to do better in the present we need to tamp down the panic. Even while we address legitimate societal and, particularly, technological risk, we need to breathe. Before you invest your (present!) hard-earned cash in an apocalypse-proof bunker or an "underground" library on a steel disk designed to outlast you, it would be good to breathe and reflect. Both help us to make rational choices and allocate resources accordingly.

I am reminded of a TV show I once saw about "doomsday preppers." In one episode, this guy lived in his underground bunker, eating canned chili for some months out of the year in order to "acclimate," or get used to living there. Thus, when things hit the fan, he could duck down and go under, psychologically happy, for as long as necessary, because he was acclimated. And he weighed about three hundred pounds.

So, it's awesome to be prepared for a crisis, and crises are possible, of course. The problem is, for this fine gentleman, his personal *health*, his physiology, was clearly a much greater risk factor than the risk of an imminent apocalypse caused by whatever. And bunker time was making one of his biggest risks still bigger. He would have been better off walking around a lot, getting more fresh vegetables. There was no *relative weighing* of the different risks. And that's what humans are bad at—not *seeing* risk, etc., but *weighing* relatively different kinds of risk. The classic one of these is that some people are so afraid of plane crashes that they drive great distances, but driving is generally much riskier than flying.

For what's the truth? What's the *real* risk of an "AI apocalypse" like the ones the movies envision for us? How do we avoid conflating "sci-fi" with "sci-*if*" (fictional sci-fi's greedy and obnoxious real-life cousin)?

TOOLS, NOT GOVERNORS

The truth is that we have no way of predicting what another "intelligence" will enable and disable in the future. It is beyond what I call the AI "event horizon." There's no data.

First, we don't even know if we can *make* another "intelligence," let alone figure out what "intelligence" is in the first place. Second, even if we could, human intelligence has never had to

deal with another "intelligence," per se, not "on par" with itself—
not at the level that the AI "optimists" are projecting.

I guess one could analogize how Neanderthals experienced
Homo sapiens back in the day, but that's not quite right. While
they may have commingled, Neanderthals didn't give rise to,
much less "design," the variant beings that more or less replaced
them. In direct contrast, artificial intelligence, if it exists, is something humans themselves *are* creating.

As Kevin Kelly (who, as it happens, has been a board member
of the Long Now Foundation), writes:

> The idea of a superhuman AI Singularity, now that it has been
> birthed, will never go away. . . . But we should recognize that it
> is a religious idea at this moment and not a scientific one. If we
> inspect the evidence we have so far about intelligence, artificial
> or natural, we can only conclude that our speculations about a
> mythical superhuman AI god are just that: myths.[2]

That is one of the themes of this book. AI is not a *Terminator*-
like race coming to destroy you; it's applied math and data. It is
something *crafted* by us—and, shortly, in particular, by *you*. Maybe it's not as "simple" as the clock of the Long Now (which is
actually pretty complicated, but definitely super cool). Certainly
AI is more ephemeral. But it's a creation, long- or short-term. And
we have to live with it. More like tools in the garage than a room-
mate.

Software automation systems are something we are very much
creating. We control them. And, again, *you*, specifically, will learn
to direct and control them—both from this book, the words and
concepts we arm you with, *and* from what you *do*. You will learn
real AI control tactics from the stuff you learn when you get to
work . . . fail . . . try again . . . fail . . . try again . . . and ultimately
succeed with your AI projects.

Neanderthal analogies aside, and even downplaying our immediate and design-based control of software systems (i.e., the
switches we can flick, as a user, and the switches we design into

the machine in the first place, as an engineer/system architect), the *Terminator* doom scenario is nowhere near this "now." As Mr. Kelly noted, current AI technology is nowhere near where the doom-mongers say; not yet, not on this beautiful day on the edge of the Golden Gate.

The thing we have to worry about now and in the foreseeable future is not exactly smart AI; it's dumb humans. I mean something really specific here in my use of the word *dumb*. It's not about intelligence. The "dumbness" I'm talking about can, and often does, arise from those who graduate at the top of their class at the best engineering schools and nerd production facilities in the world. In fact, sometimes the most educated people are most likely to meet my definition here. What I mean by "dumb" in this instance is any of the following characteristics: careless; arrogant; selfish; greedy. Arrogantly careless? Greedily arrogant? Hubristic?

AI that is "dumb," or that gets the dumbness "baked in" from inception, in this sense, is only "dumb" because a human was arrogant or hubristic in programming it, or setting it loose upon the Internet, etc. It's hubris that we're worried about, because that's the kind of thing we've seen so much of in Silicon Valley (said with love) over the last twenty years or so. And this is precisely where *you* can be smarter than the others, smarter than AI, the nerds, and far more than either: commonsensical.

In other words, *it's not the "cars," but the "czars"* that are the more-immediate threat to life, limb, and even employment! What do we have to worry about this second? It's the all-too-human creators and drivers of AI, the all-too-flawed flesh, the greed-obsessed brains—those that have fallen so much in love with their own technical progress that they lose sight of their societal outcomes. Bad drivers of automation, designers and managers of AI who race to meet their engineering project management deadlines, their releases, their ad revenue targets, their grant deadlines, etc., without regard to bystanders or bystander data. *Bad or nonexistent AI "governors" are the most immediate problem.*

This is not a new conundrum, people! Martin Luther King Jr. saw it. He described a country, and a world, of "guided missiles and misguided men." John F. Kennedy also saw it. He noted, in talking about space and space exploration, that science was neither good nor evil. Human beings had to invest themselves to use those tools for one or the other. Science, engineering, are just vessels. We can fill and direct them for good and evil as we see fit, and we judge the results.

It's not as if all of you will be using AI to "fight evil." Some of you may just be making money (without exploiting others, naturally), and that's just fine. But even so, you need to appreciate some of the excesses and extremes we have already started to see in this pearl-like instance of time on the edge of the Bay.

You can help *fix* it. You can help fix broken software code, even if you are not the one to write it. As the founders of the United States intuited in their very stable "code" document (i.e., the US Constitution), you have more common sense than anyone who just thinks about 1s and 0s. Nerds of all stripes and in all menageries have their place, but that place is not always in the driver's seat of the technology they themselves created for love or profit. They do not always have *perspective*. Engineering does not determine direction. Direction, destination of the vessel, that is a policy question—and that is where you come in, whatever your goal is.

Direction (along with some other stuff, including maybe design, evaluation, etc.) is your job, as the controller of your technical destiny, your data, and your job itself.

The fundamental fallacy of AI nerdery is that it presumes it knows best how to regulate itself. But *no one* knows how to regulate oneself: not nerds, not AI, not anybody or anything. There is no software code that can completely understand the universe, and there are limits to the completeness of any mathematical system. We are biased, and we are blinkered when it comes to thinking about our own biases. We are like wheels out of alignment that need an outside force to "true up," be it government or an external code. The "self-regulation" concept fails in companies and it fails in societies. It must be led. AI must be "steered." It must be balanced.

SECURITY IS A DESIGN PROBLEM

You have probably heard of cybertheft? Similar issue. Similar outcome (as much as we love the Internet . . . *most* of the time).

Cybersecurity is a design problem. The original engineering for the Internet, most computation, and most computational devices (in fact, most *communications networks on Earth*, period), didn't necessarily grasp the reality that most modern technology, the "Internet Superhighway," etc., was also going to become the super-*theft*, super-*fraud* highway, the crypto-tragic high-speed rail of organized crime, child pornography, and terrorism, the Hate Net. The "Make Sure I See No Opinions But My Own" Robot Network, the Internet of intellectual auto-erotica.

Not every other actor on the Internet is bad, of course. Most folks are . . . just folks, but there is a nasty minority of network exploitation leveraged by some of the worst, most hateful, most criminal, most petty, and most parasitic aspects of society: those who exploit the naive, the unguarded, the weak, and—well, heck, most of us. No one is really unexposed. And those with technological leverage can cause much greater harm, at much greater speed than in the old days, in some ways.

Really, to be done right, security has to be *designed* into communications and computation networks, not added on as an afterthought, as has happened for most of modern history. Anyone with street smarts could have predicted that this thing was going to be used, if for highly scalable commerce and communication, then also for theft on a highly networked and at least semi-automated scale.

But the problem is that the Internet—like the phone system, once upon a time—was a bright shiny thing, a goal in its own right, and designed to maximize communication among nodes. It was hard just to build it in the first place, to get the "talkie" happening. What an amazing day that was, to get the phone working, the "talking telegraph"! Those folks were not thinking about criminal usage. To be clear, I don't think this is a problem with how we "invent." I think this is a problem with how we *productize*, with how we turn cool inventions into mass market tools and systems used by millions of people.

Such communications networks, and the computational infrastructure that followed, were *not* designed to detect and prevent theft and other wrongdoing. They were not designed to self-detect, deter, or punish bad folks roaming its electron streams with impunity. And so—surprise, surprise—they don't! Essentially we just have a bunch of Band-Aids on a broken levy.

The fundamental problem was (and still is, for AI) that not everyone in charge of designing such systems *had* (or cared about) street smarts. We love the shiny. We love to create. And sometimes that shine leads us to forget the reality, the whims and tendencies of human nature. *We are so eager to make the connection that we forget to build the filter*, to control, to let the good electrons in but block the bad. In other words (and I say this *as* a nerd): *Where the nerd runs free, the common sense runs away.*

Engineering requirements, technical "magic," and need for speed for profit, have historically come way above and before future theft prevention. Effectuating the magic has come long before any long-term common sense . . . much less a "long now." And maybe this is why I think this bar—I mean, that idea about long-term thinking—is so important for us designing AI *today.*

"Cybersecurity" shouldn't be needed. We should have built better network control systems into our communications architecture. We didn't think long-term enough, and we're doing it again! The "Internet of Things"? The fridge that talks to you, and talks to your toaster, which talks to the supermarket to order more eggs and toast (or whatever nerd-food replacement in a vat we are going to be ingesting in two to three years)? Virtually none of that stuff is secured. It's going to be yet another means of home data theft. Already is, to some extent. Don't get me wrong; I'm not hating the toaster, nor even the autonomous toaster. I'm just questioning priorities.

Engineering requirements come first. "Cool" came first, and it still does. The hazy, but inevitable (to a commonsense intelligence) future problems get sandblasted and whitewashed by the "cool," by the short-term profit. And we get a snazzy new object that automates access to our privacy and our homes, by the good, yes, but sometimes by the bad and the ugly electrons.

We do *not* want AI to follow this same pattern. It's too big, too powerful, too scalable. It builds and will eventually help teach itself. So the code we program into its guts has got to be solid, and has got to consider human law and (as embodied in that law) human security and optimization. Isaac Asimov, a brilliant scientist and sci-fi author, knew this. And that's why he proposed the "laws of robotics," decades before real AI, which prioritized human welfare.

I like to quote a little religious adage to drive my AI management (among other things): *The beginning of wisdom is the fear of G-d.* Let me just translate that into "hard data" for those averse to religion:

a. The set of things we know is always vastly exceeded by the set of things we *don't* know. *Corollary to "A":* The more we learn, the more experience we accrete, the more we understand the truth of "A."

b. Assume all data are false until proven otherwise. These are magical amulets, these little phrases, that are going to help you at all times during your sojourn in the land of OZ . . . I mean, AI.

And with those in your pocket, let us lay out some basic predilections/principles about "AI predictions." These stem from the above: *Humans are notoriously bad at predicting the future.* So, unlike almost every futurist author with a "pot o' gold" lucky leprauchan or "prophet-in-a-pocket" syndrome, we *won't.*

For example, we won't predict anywhere in this book how far AI is going to go, or how soon, or how deadly to humanity it could be (or when we actually need to be concerned about "self-aware" AI). Even if we could predict something like that, it's unlikely to help you in *today's* now, which is all we have. (Remember, your bunker budget is limited, and you have at least one belly to feed.) No prediction.

So, today: What to do about cybertheft (designed or misdesigned-in insecurity) and AI Nerdageddon?! You can't really see the full scope of the risk, but we know for *certain* that bad and even malignant drivers of technology exist.

WHAT TO DO? TWO THINGS, PLUS EDEN

One: Plan for the long term now. Don't make dumb, short-term choices because it's "cool" or, conversely, out of panic. Design for at least the medium term, if not the long term.

But, *two*: live like you've only got today, and the data you have today. Don't drive yourself crazy about what AI could be in twenty years. Because, the truth is (again, see above), humans are notoriously bad at predicting the future. You will need AI (read: a lot of data, applied mathematical tools, software, and hardware) to help manage and make AI's future.

One plus two equals: Learn like crazy, including about the technical stuff, but don't *be* crazy. Don't fall for a bunch of jargon, or a bunch of AI snake-oil marketing speak. Focus on the practical outcomes of these projects.

Your common sense is a unique asset to steer, design, and manage even the most complex AI projects. At the very least, your common sense will help you ask good questions of the nerds you are working with. It's not magic. If you don't know about, or can't directly manage, the tech, ask about/manage the technicians.

We can call the above axioms *strategic* tools. They help you think about the big picture. Why you are doing stuff. What the project is for. But let's get a little more detailed, a little more "tactical." As mentioned above, we will arm you with a recipe, a recipe for mixing and "baking" AI. It's called EDEN, which is short for "Empirical, Design, Evolution, Net." More specifically, EDEN is a recipe for designing, developing, evaluating, maintaining, and improving AI platforms. Like a good cake recipe, EDEN leverages your skill and perspective as a "user" (read: "eater"), among other things. Much like a cake, you *cannot* unbake an AI platform that has already scaled—especially if it involves deep learning or other opaque and sometimes inscrutable causal machinery behind its behavior or classification scheme. It's too late! The cake is a new kind of thing different from its components alone. You can only improve it, or bake a new one.

EDEN and other tools in this book are all *adaptive*. (Again: We don't assume we can predict the future. In fact, we assume we can't.) They should serve you no matter what comes. That is what you need. Even a hyper technical toolkit about coding and assembling AI platforms will get outdated practically from the time these words hit the printers, if not before. We give you leads, but the tech and the tools are evolving, generally in your favor. In fact, the tech is generally getting easier to apply, with (somewhat) less effort and expertise. Systems are being made easier and easier to use, including by nontechnical people.

As the tech user interface evolves and simplifies, you gain more advantages. Whereas once AI companies had all the cards, now there is more than one good AI services provider and lots of open source code. Whereas once such companies were, in some ways, commoditizing *you* (as a user, project owner, and even as a consumer), now you can commoditize *them*.

That being said, the axioms above, as well as EDEN and the other practical tools in this system, are things you need to not just learn, but apply and *train* on. You need to *train* to leverage and manage AI, to avoid becoming roadkill on the road to Nerdvana.

Now.

It's time.

GOVERNING AI—KUBERNETES / CONTROL SYSTEMS

I know everyone likes delicious baked goods. But first, before we get to the recipe, a word . . . on a word. Specifically, the word *cyber*. I used it above. Hear it a lot, eh? But what does it mean?

Sounds like magic or something? It's not. Yet it conceals a vast mystery that's going to help you: a wrong turn in the dark corridors and the abyss of nerdery . . . in a place called Greece, or MIT, or some time-bound conflation of the two.

Cyber, cybernetic, and *cyberspace* are commonly used to refer to computer networks (generally), like the Internet. *Cyborg* is also used to refer to a human-computer amalgam (the "centaur" of our prospective future, so to speak). *Cyberspace* was a concept first used by the brilliant sci-fi author William Gibson, to refer to Internet interactions as a kind of alternate reality, into which humans could, using virtual reality body suits, "plug in."

But . . . want to be let in on a little secret? It's totally wrong.

Cybernetic was never supposed to mean "computer network." It got drafted into an army of common misusages and jargon—the same dang pattern of lexical misadventure and hubris (Greek word for extreme pride or "pride before the fall") that gave us the overwrought and historically self-defeating term *artificial intelligence*!

The roots of the word *cybernetics* actually go back to ancient Greece, so let's travel there right now. *Cybernetic* comes from *kubernetes,* which is a Greek word that means "steering mechanism" or "steersman." For example, it can refer to the tiller or other mechanical means for "governing" a ship. Greek philosophers first started using the metaphor of the steering oarsman to refer to guiding the ship of state. *Kubernetes* translated into Latin is "gubernetes," which gives us "governor."

But away from memory and back to modern times: Invented by an MIT professor named Norbert Wiener, modern *cybernetics* was originally *the science of communication and control systems— mechanical, biological, or political.* Wiener didn't really differentiate between the complex biological control system regulating hunger and satiety, the automatic control system that helps to keep modern high-speed trains on tracks, and systems of human governance. He believed they were mathematically parallel and one could learn and productively reapply from one domain to another. Wiener was a pioneer of modern computer science, but his cybernetics study, sadly, became unpopular among other nerds.

Too much common sense?

Lesson one: You need to be thinking in terms of *control systems* for the AI platforms you and your companies are building. Even if you are not in the guts of the mechanics of the AI, you need to be aware of how it is being used, what gets communicated into—and out of—it, and related matter. You do not need to *be* the ship. You need not know *all* of its technical construction details (though that can be helpful). But you *do* need to be the governor, the helmsman. Without you, the ship will run aground. Never let anyone tell you differently.

More practically said: You need to wisely "steer" these AI projects, or they will rapidly fall away from their intended project goals and spin you into the rocks. It's a simple message, but should be emphasized: *Be cybernetic.* You are the governor of your company's AI projects. They do not govern you. They have no will, nor any intention. You must provide both, and constantly tend to the data—for the data are the wind and the waves of your environment.

This is so simple a message that I feel like a dummy for writing it. You would think the above would be obvious and all engineers would know it, as well as all executives.

And you would be wrong.

They don't. Engineers are taught how to build stuff. They aren't necessary taught how to wisely "steer" or "govern." Even old Norbert had a hard time pushing cybernetics theory at his own school. Intellectually, his cybernetics got stuffed into a school locker, by the other nerds. So it is up to you to design and maintain AI control systems—whether they are embedded in technology or the people you are managing. That is not a technical function, but rather a policy one.

"OUTSMARTING" AI MEANS LEVERAGING AI

It's not really true that you can "outsmart" AI, meaning "out-reckon" it, any more than you can "outrun" a car or "outfly" an airplane. You can't. But you can *steer* an airplane (or decide which plane you are going to take, and to where). You can drive a car (until the ninnies make that illegal too). You can navigate using, or leveraging, either, to get where you want to go, faster than you could by flapping away on your own.

What's different between AI and a physical transportation mo-dality (like a car, a plane, or an ancient Greek ship) is that it costs, basically, zero to make one more copy of the identical AI. It's software. Zip! Zap! Done. Copying the software costs nothing, or close enough to zero that it practically is. It may well take you resources and time to establish or adopt useful AI for your own ends. That "development" cost may be quite substantial, both in organizational, data tagging, and technical development time. We call that time, and those initial development resources, a "fixed cost."

But copying the AI has a real cost of zero (no matter how many times), and it costs zero to use it one more time. Let me sum up:

1. AI has a high fixed cost of development (and, generally, of initial application);
2. AI has a low or zero marginal cost of copying and, particu-larly, additional usage (each subsequent "transaction" or computational action).

Those are magical artifacts. Remember this adage, and use it always. It will help inform how and where you develop and *specify* AI projects and platforms. It will help you figure out value vs. risk/cost for these things.

By way of example, let's focus on consumer voice recognition projects. Giant software services companies have spent hundreds of millions of dollars developing software that a) leverages even *greater* investments by others in data, communications networks, computer hardware, etc.; and b) recognizes your voice (sometimes) and takes an action that you tell it to do (most of the time). ("Hey X, play some music." "Hey X, order me a cheeseburger." "Hey X, what's the weather today? Is it cheeseburger weather?")

In addition to the expense, these giant companies have leveraged trillions of economic infrastructure to achieve the pinnacle of human civilization's achievement: the ability to order a cheeseburger without moving from your hot tub. However, while all that investment happened, it costs them essentially *zero* to carry out the "brain work" of "understanding" your speech and sending it to "Mr. Burger" or "Ms. Weather Summarizer." High fixed cost. Essentially zero marginal cost.

It's more complicated in real life than in an economics textbook. We'll revisit this, but that gets you the basics you need for now: AI has high fixed cost, low marginal cost. *But one last thing*: Burger/music/weather ordering is one thing. Those machines / AI platforms (hardware and software included, essentially) are not quite so good at: "Write me a sonnet" or "Make my child less grumpy." The things, the specific tasks, that AI is good with today (and our foreseeable tomorrow) need to be *repeatable and standardizable*. AI can't figure out common sense, or human emotion, or even "grumpy." "Grumpy AI" is as out of reach, for the present "now," as "Commonsense AI."

AS ABOVE, SO BELOW: TWO NERD LANGUAGES

You will notice that I am using more than one type of "nerd language." Brennan typically winces when I use nerd words, and I *have* tried to limit their usage. But you will need to learn both these languages, *to some extent*, because certain nerd verbiage helps you organize real-life concepts and projects. Just as mathematical notation helps mathematicians solve problems with less thought/work, so will these words automatically help you navigate AI project management.

The first nerd lingo is "Silicon Valley." 'Nuff said. Unless you know that, the engineers you may need to talk to won't respect you, or give you the time of day (unlike the AIs they may be creating; see above). They shall remain grumpy. Silicon Valley language is all over the place. You probably already know that you need to learn the basic concepts thoroughly, just to ask good questions and *design* good projects (and even more so, to *execute* them successfully).

The second nerd lingo is "law and economics." This second nerd language—learned by me with vastly more pain and suffering than I am inflicting on you via this sentence—gives you concepts like, above: "fixed cost, marginal cost" and, below: "network effects."

These languages are like software code that illuminate the reality behind the Wizard of Oz—I mean, the AI projects. Use them well. "There's no place like home. . . . There's no place like home. . . . There's no place like home."

NETWORK EFFECTS FOR BIG DATA

So, in addition to featuring high fixed cost and low marginal cost, AI generally gets *better* every time a user interacts with it (e.g., clicks a button or enters some data). The way you say "cheeseburger" or "weather," a thousand different ways, then have to correct the AI when it orders you a "cheese booger" instead (these things are real!), feeds back into the data pipeline, and corrects back to the model. The "model" or "language model" is the ontological ("computery") structure the machine uses to calibrate and correlate:

a. the sounds you are spouting (from under your hot tub's surface); and

b. the concept of the word *cheeseburger*, or *weather*, or X (whatever it is the AI platform needs to "translate" into an action). (We'll address later how the AI differentiates your word-sound bubbles from other bubbles.)

Good AI "learns" from all the data, which comes from its use (as well as feedback about its success, etc., for each analytic operation). So, to revise our metaphor: *AI is like an airplane that gets faster, more efficient, and more comfortable the more it is used*—a kind of anti-maintenance algorithm. If you start such a flight from Houston to Toronto at 300 miles per hour, by the time you fly over Memphis you're at Mach 3! And your flight flipped from peanuts to a five-course French meal, with live entertainment (cancan dancers and so forth), at the same time. (The unused plane, in contrast, becomes a relatively slower way to travel, less economically useful, less user-friendly, and eventually turns into [relative] junk. Tough market!)

In fact, this "AI airplane" is even better than that! It gets better not just every time *it* flies. It gets better every time one of its twenty thousand clone airplanes flies. It shares data with its friend airplanes, like the Borg in *Star Trek* (named for "cyborg," which term goes back to, you guessed it: Socrates and Mr. Wiener. We too, as humans, can talk to each other, even across time—just like Socrates talked to Captain Picard). Put back into a real-life context: Each piece of implemented AI software in a network, "hockey pucks," talks to its clone hockey pucks, and/or the central AI platform.

Talk about efficient innovation!

Stocked, as they are, with these super-duper, self-improving auto-networked "AI airplanes" that acceleratingly outclass their less-used peers: You see how a successful Silicon Valley company can come to dominate very quickly. They only need one big automated software hit, then a) they can sell/adapt the tool to an unlimited number of people, at potentially huge profit; b) the massive release to large numbers of people creates massively more data, which makes the AI way better than before—*"acceleratingly" better*—and, therefore, c) their lead becomes self-sustaining.

The lead of a successful software company over its peers, or the old market, looks not like a hockey puck, but like a hockey *stick*: When the advantage starts to rise past a certain point, it spikes rapidly up. In fact, venture capitalists look for this hockey stick projection in the investment pitches they get, both in a company's financial model *and* in their user data and technical transaction patterns.

That's why you can't be a passive observer ("nerdserver"?) in the AI economy. The gap between you and the economic leaders will expand at a compounding rate. You have to participate. How do you steer a self-improving, self-dominating airplane, especially if the model has been built by someone else?

This same math, the math we outlined above—*the compounding network effects of AI, the high fixed and low marginal cost of AI*—can work in your favor, if you have a unique data set or analytic bent (i.e., a hard creativity or a unique situation). But you have to get started. You can't be a bystander on the road to AI, because there is no safe place for a bystander to stand.

That means getting your hands dirty right now. You have to break through a wall of what seems like impenetrable math or "magic" (to most of us that might have meant the same thing for most of high school; I remember!). You have to dive into the actual data, the math (or some high-level understanding of it), the text (no excuses)—the qualitative and quantitative nuance of what these platforms actually are. Stand up, and steer yourself.

To press this point further: You have to simply destroy the idea that there is anything called "AI" at all. There is just raw data, and software-instantiated math. The rest is mythology. Leave that to the Greeks.

ON BUILDING AI

Data is the Mother of AI. Math is the Father. (Recall rules #1 and #2 in chapter 1.)

But if data are so important, why do they get such short shrift in most practical applications? No one thinks about data when designing their grand plans, but the original data sets are the grounds, the matrix, the essence from which the success or failure of most AI projects derives. Even one of the heads of IBM's AI business has noted that "about 80 percent of the work with an AI project is collecting and preparing data."[3]

People think a bunch of fancy software is going to solve all their problems for them, with *no work* on their part. But that's not true. Software doesn't even know what to do (again, no human being at the helm) unless it's given a very specific target/destination, generally speaking. *It certainly can't fix chaos*, if you give it chaos, and nothing more. It can't tell you where to go. It can't fix sloppy data. You generally have to navigate—and curate—your own data. These are big projects.

Reality is much messier than the mythology, or even the experience of a consumer with basic AI tools. You can't fix crazy data without highly sane technical specifications. You can't fix unwisdom with good algorithms. You can't fix bad design with world-class math. You can't fix garbage data with algorithms descending from heaven (or Silicon Valley). If anyone tells you different, don't believe them.

WHAT IT TAKES TO MAKE AI "MAGIC"

Let's go back to that magical AI software that listens to your voice ("chaotic"), interprets your words "accurately" (more or less), and then follows your instructions (specific, orderly action).

The reality on the front end is bedlam. It takes millions and millions of dollars and a lot of "ordering," a lot of control, before software like that becomes practically useful. It didn't interpret your bubbles successfully, even some of the time, without a lot of other work that (mostly) happened well in advance of your cheese-burger-less submergence.

That kind of AI software has to intake every type of audio data imaginable—from background noise, to a zillion different accents, to "X" number of languages, to "N" different word sounds—which even an individual person speaks at least a little differently every time. How is that "chaos" turned into relatively accurate AI software that does what you ask it to?

Humans! Tens of thousands of humans, all over the world, tag and un-tag every little word, from certain audio samples of every type of word, and accent, the AI needs to process. Then they do it again. Then they do it again. Then they do it again.

You get the idea.

And through this extremely un-neat, highly iterative process, the AI gets a little better at "listening" and "interpreting" the sounds of humans speaking words. It's messy as heck. And it takes a whole honkin' organized infrastructure, and a lot of kludging around with raw data, to make something simple, some "magic AI," out of something chaotic. (And then there's the issue of who has legal rights to all that sound! Oi. See below.)

These software machines aren't magic at all. That "automation" is fed, nurtured, and "educated" by a vast array of highly orchestrated social understanding and business infrastructure. The Great and Powerful AI, like the Wizard of Oz, is really just the apex, the surface level, of a lot of human kludging around, behind the scenes.

Yes, there is technology and "gearing systems" behind the scenes to make the human work of tagging and reclassifying data efficient. Yes, that technology is getting better and may even semi-automate this stuff. Yes, there are efforts to make AI more "effortless" in application. But in this now, the secret ingredient to a lot of practical AI is human work.

We're going to train you, at a high level, on how to do that kludging among the best of them—for fun, progress, and profit. If there is "magic," it should belong to you, and your company, not Internet giants, not governments, not the nerds.

THE EDEN METHOD

As mentioned, EDEN (Empirical, Design, Evolution, Net) is a method of designing, building, maintaining, and improving AI platforms. But unlike a cake recipe, these things do not necessarily have to be done in that order. That is, EDEN is nonlinear. You may want to do "design" first, for instance, even though it's listed second. Other things, like "net," and "evolution" are things you are doing regularly, like feeding a child. *In other words, EDEN is a nonlinear recipe for "baking" enterprise-grade AI.*

EDEN is not necessarily about the super-technical or project-specific steps you need to take in order to engineer an AI system. Instead, it tells you the what, why, and how of AI. It teaches you to be a good parent, or AI manager.

Empirical means to start with a very reliable empirical data set. By "reliable," I mean data that are a) accurate, and b) reflect or measure things that actually happened. Empirical data should be as objective as possible; that is, they are usually the *opposite* of opinions (unless you are gathering EMPIRICAL data about totally subjective statements by humans [*five out of ten people in Buffalo at X time stated that they believe it will not snow this winter . . .* that sort of thing]).

For example, empirical data may include the number and types of lawsuits filed in the United States, as well as their specific legal outcomes. Another example is the number of financial transactions in the United Kingdom as of time period X–Y. (You'll notice there is a bit of a legal tone or tendency to my empirical definition. There's a reason for that.) Other empirical data could include a) the number of meteorites hitting the atmosphere in a given period of time, b) the number of bat rays in the canals of San Francisco in May of a given year, or c) the total number of eggplants grown in a specific Japanese farm over a ten-year period.

Empirical can include social or legal transactions, as well as material things. It's all data. But opinions? No. You and I and AI are focused on events. Hard data. We may be certain or uncertain about these events (and usually this is a matter of degree). But they happened / will happen, or did not / will not.

Cosmologist Carl Sagan gives us a pretty good description of what we mean by "empirical," above, even if AI engineering and management is not really a science. (Cosmology, btw, is the study of stars and large-scale cosmic phenomena. Carl did other stuff, too, but we know him most for the universals.) As he wrote in *The Skeptical Inquirer*:

> Science is much more than a body of knowledge. It is a way of thinking. This is central to its success. Science invites us to let the facts in, even when they don't conform to our preconceptions [read "opinions"!]. It counsels us to carry alternative hypotheses in our heads and see which ones best match the facts. It urges on us a fine balance between no-holds-barred openness to new ideas, however heretical, and the most rigorous skeptical scrutiny of everything—new ideas and established wisdom. We need wide appreciation of this kind of thinking. It works. It's an essential tool for a democracy in an age of change.[4]

In addition to being a tool for democracy, it's also an essential tool for developing AI, particularly if that AI somehow affects humans. And, speaking of humans . . .

Design means design with the end user foremost in your mind. This user is the type of person or actual individual you are building the system for. This doesn't mean you have to consider all the *beneficiaries* of your AI, just the users. (For example, if your AI helps parents gather healthy food, their entire family may *benefit*. But the *user* of your system is a parent.)

To put this in slightly more formal terms, the "goal" of your system is primarily directed at solving the user's problem or carrying out specific user tasks. You design by a) identifying who the user (or user type) is; and b) what she needs. The AI platform is designed to carry out that goal—solve that user problem, or handle that user request.

Who is she or he? Is it you (trying to help you do something better, faster, cheaper, like a Japanese cucumber farmer)? Or is the system or its outputs going to be used by someone else?

Figure this stuff out—*Who is the user? What is her pain/need? What does the platform need to accomplish to address that need/ pain?*—before all else. Measure your progress against those definitions—always. Your empathy will correlate directly to your success. If you can't understand a user's/patient's/buyer's pain, you will not succeed in selling to them either. So, listen, and focus on them beyond all else.

Evolution is not a political statement. It means that your system needs to constantly evolve to stay relevant, popular, and as accurate as reasonably possible. Essentially all AI platforms need to be constantly re-tuned, based on new data, including new user inputs and demands. Some AI programs are self-tuning, but for our purposes, let's assume you (and/or your project team) are going to need to stay involved.

Don't think you're done. Ever. AI is a cake that needs to be constantly "re-baked" and retested. Or, to "remix" the batter (or my metaphors): An AI is "a living document," a data-mathematical organism. If you don't feed and tend to it, it will die (or, worse, live on, zombie-like, with increasingly error-ridden days and outputs— even destructive outputs).

Net means you will need to sum multiple factors to get to a single answer.

Let's lay out an example: When you get a search result on the Internet, a search engine uses many, many features to rank or express a single list of (hopefully) the most relevant answers. The classes of data it uses may include:

1. the text you entered in the search box (obv.); but also
2. the location you are searching from;
3. the things you've clicked through to in the past;
4. what other people tend to click on when they searched for similar words;
5. yada yada yada.

It's not simply one thing. It "weights" a lot of different data objects, so maybe your text/search request string is 60 percent of the search result weight, but a lot of other things go into a best-in-class search result set, too. Your location could be 2 percent of the ranking algorithm for that search request. What happened that day could be 10 to 20 percent (e.g., if a big thing in the news or other event made it more likely that a search word meant you were looking for that thing). Alternatively, we give weights to how other people cited different search result pages (and how much we trust those other people). We weight each of these things to compile into a single ranking of search results called a "feature."

For EDEN, and AI project management purposes, the things we are netting can get pretty complicated, but the goal is to get to the exact, nuanced thing the user is trying to achieve. We "net" different factors and features to get there. We synthesize and summarize. We are going to apply all four of the above elements of EDEN, very specifically, in chapter 6.

ON DATA CONTROL

It's a beautiful Sunday again in San Francisco, part of Fleet Week, with the bay full of white sails and a scattering of navy vessels— along with the usual array of freighters, scows, ferries, and sometimes visible sea creatures cruising under and over the waves.

More sonically relevant: The Blue Angels Navy Demonstration team is performing outside my window. (Well, not *just* for me. *Mostly*, but not entirely. There is also that whole other city/planet. But who's counting?) It's got me thinking airplanes.

Remember our conversation about self-improving airplanes? You take off in Memphis and—behold!—the plane is faster and more efficient by the time you come in to land.

This auto-improving plane is just a metaphor for AI. Once it is properly built, there is a feedback loop in the machine: The system keeps improving itself. Well-founded AI systems improve at a compounding rate, with use, including any use by a deployed piece of software (i.e., a "node") within the same computer network. Every "hockey puck" AI chatbot in a home will *ultimately* learn from every other "hockey puck" of the same brand / computer network.

So let's summarize our self-learning on self-learning AI.

- *Zero marginal cost* (for each piece of new software, and each additional operation of any node in the system),
- *Compounding improvements*, and, relatedly
- *Network effects*, mean that AI and similar "big data" platforms can improve and gain more or less dominating leads over their competing systems.

Oh yeah, one more thing about that confounded compounded set of things:

- It costs "zero" for one additional copy of the software, and "zero" (or *less* than zero, since it's useful) for one more operation of that AI software, but I can *charge* the same amount for every single operation.
- Let's do the math: It effectively costs $10 for a newcomer to run each AI software operation/action, and it can charge $10 per answer/whatever output required. This is mostly because you have to allocate the fixed cost of building it to your ultimate user group.
- For an operation with much greater scale, it may cost $3 for each user operation (I can sell ads for each user, *and* I get an AI feature improvement benefit for every use, which outside investors see, so they amp my company's market value), but I can still *sell* each AI operation for $10.
- This means the profit variance between Company One and Company Two is (One: $0, Two: $10 + $3) net $13.00.
- In reality, most big AI companies charge $0 for AI operations, and upsell on other things, leveraging their user base / data reservoir and resultant AI advantages. (More on this later—but you get the idea.)

- Titanic AI platforms have a weird economic feature in that, in theory, marginal costs can fall to below zero even as pricing power stays static (or even increases).

What's the nerd word for that? Oh yeah. The same phrase as the non-nerd term: *Money Machine.* AI changing the world? Oh yeah. And also Silicon Valley checking account balances.

THE "U" IN "AI"

In this vein, what do you have that is unique that can be used (for "fun, profit, or progress") in a world where big-enterprise AI systems can dominate?

One: Your data.

Two: Your creativity.

Three: Your control and focus over both.

Let me give you yet another a real-life example. (I knowww!! *Too real, dude!*) Back in ye olden days, the music industry had a "monopoly"—to some degree—over how music got consumed and, to a lesser extent, the medium in which those works were recorded. If you wanted to buy access to a song (the right to listen to that one song when you wanted to), you had to buy an entire album. The right to that one song was "tied" to those other songs, and you had to buy the set. Even before that, buying a "single" on a vinyl disc required you to buy at least one more side (A/B).

Then, the Internet happened. People started ripping and mixing songs, and sharing them with each other, including total strangers, at will. The music industry did not especially like this, so they killed off the biggest network platform for music sharing, Napster, and sued thousands of consumers for file sharing, successfully arguing that they were violating copyrights of creators and publishers.

The music industry prevailed on many of their copyright claims, yes, but, on the other hand, they failed to take advantage of the possibilities the Internet entailed. They failed to deliver on the new potential utilities the Internet presented to their clients, the users/buyers/public. Instead, they sued them. *No soup for you! Just more lawyers!!*

Suffice it to say: The industry was *not* user-oriented as a whole. It was past-oriented, album preservation–oriented. There were many opportunities the Internet offered for new products, features, and even profits. But a defensive view prevailed. As I was wont to say at the time: *It is perhaps the first time in history when you can lose your pants by holding onto them too tightly.*

Now, as it happens—and lest you think I am unfairly picking on the billionaire music moguls of yore—the *mainline legal industry in the United States is in almost exactly the same forensic position that the music industry was during the Napster era.* We have lots of legal start-ups, and lots of cool tech happening in the space, and most of it is *not* happening inside traditional law firms, despite all the pressure their users/clients are putting on them. The "good" news for law firms is that law firm enterprise clients tend to be somewhat more empowered (and, shall we say, "listenable") than Susie Johnson, thirteen, who just *really* needs to hear "Girls Just Wanna Have Fun" without the rest of the album.

Lesson? If you have a legal monopoly (like a copyright, or a registration bar / professional license requirement), don't abuse it. Stay client-focused. Evolve in ways that help your clients (including use of AI and tech). Or your clients will ultimately undo you.

For, in music: Users had had a taste of the future, and they were unwilling to go back to the past, back to the box (or the boxed set), even if the leading music-sharing platform of the day, Napster, had been eviscerated and turned into lawyer confetti.

Users just went underground.

Revenues for the industry as a whole continued to crater.

Creators continued to not get paid much, especially the new folks.

And the music industry *still, still* hasn't recovered from that moment in history. Steve Jobs was actually one of the first people to really address this problem, via the original iTunes deals, but he caught a lot of heck for it from the feds. Ditto for analogous book publishing deal discussions. Full disclosure (and this is public info), Apple was a buyer of my data at my first start-up, Lex Machina, so maybe I'm conflicted. But I believe what I wrote above personally, in no small part because the music and book publishing industries were essentially "failing," getting creamed by large online distribution platforms. To avoid failing completely, or being commoditized, they needed market leverage, to wit: transactions that allowed them to access Internet network distribution platforms at scale, platforms that partnered with them.

However, someone else—also in the greater Los Angeles region—was watching this music industry fiasco, this multiyear train wreck of law, technology-sundered distribution networks, and music industry egos: the audiovisual industry—moviemakers, show makers, Internet distribution platforms. Producers said to themselves: *If we wait too long, until Internet connections are fast enough to stream audiovisual content, we will also get hammered. Just like the music industry.* (If you know your history, you are less likely to repeat it, people. As Santayana/Churchill liked to say, more or less.)

On the other side of the California—the top part—companies like Netflix (and particularly *that* company) realized that online video distribution was going to happen, needed to happen, for them to increase their profit margins, versus being in the business of mailing back and forth a jillion physical DVDs. Both producers and distributors wanted to avoid the ongoing music industry fiasco. Was there a "win-win"?

Indeed.

"I'll take 'YES' for a thousand, Alex."

We saw what we *hadn't* seen in the music industry at that equivalent moment in time: *Massive innovation/evolution. New platforms. New deals with Internet bigs.* Now, at time of writing, there is *massive spending* on new audiovisual content, and big distributors fight fiercely for consumer eyeballs and subscription dollars by paying premiums for top content creation. It is not necessarily that "content is king," but, even independent or small-scale audiovisual content creators are massively better off, when mapped or viewed against the equivalent time stream, compared to musicians.

Two lessons for the AI / "big data" revolution: First, hiding in a shell, lashing out at innovation, is only going to *reduce* the value of your unique data, creativity, and focus. Lesson two: Internet giants are trying to commoditize you (extract your data so that it makes their AI "hum," and be better and faster than everybody else's). You need to commoditize *them*. As of today (and, hopefully, your today): There are several AI giants competing for your time, money, and attention. Be like the A/V people, the creators in particular, not like the music producers. Make the AI giants compete for you and your works, even for your personal data. Giving away your personal data for a few technical "baubles" is like losing your technology marbles. Don't do it.

Discipline. Discipline, people.

This is true of you as a consumer, as well as you as an AI manager. More on the latter now. You have to be the moth that does not seek out the flame. You have to have discipline in every part of your business and in every "data-related" contract you sign. Who owns the improvements? How do you know that your partner is complying, and not taking your creative or competitive advantage for themselves?

What if the data, creativity, and focus of consumer types are already captured by a big third party? As with countries, so too with companies. Any monopoly power will inevitably be abused. It is human nature. A government in power will inevitably abuse its own citizens to maintain such power and authority. A sufficiently powerful technological network will also abuse its power, if left unchecked. They're the same. One power is cross-leveraged to maximize another power, to achieve greater economic monopolies, citizenry control, etc.

Thus, extreme libertarianism and totalitarianism inevitably lead to the same result: In the former case, network competition victors can parlay early victories into economic dominance, and cross-leverage domination in one area to gain domination in another corporate sector. In antitrust terms, this is called "tying." Alternatively, with a sufficiently cohesive club or coalition in a single economic sector, "trusts" can be arranged to reduce competition. (Again, competition is essentially the opposite of monopoly.)

Totalitarianism likewise abuses its limited monopoly over the use of force to kill a) term limits, b) opponents, and c) hope.

The truth is, those charged with guarding against monopolies are themselves relying on a monopoly power. One may be as dangerous, or worse, than the other. There's no forensic analytic way to tell this in advance. You just have to weigh and counterweigh the good, the bad, and the ugly of the application of monopoly rights. For example, it is argued that the anti-monopoly enforcers of Europe are just anti-American—leveraging their "save the people" rhetoric to be anti-competitive themselves, giving local companies an unjust leg up.

The Jains are a religious group originating in India, and they have a proverb that goes: *When you hate, you hate yourself.* The lesson is that people often project the worst of themselves on others, "out groups," or leverage the *fear* of something atrocious to *commit* atrocity. This happens all over, throughout the world, in many, many time periods, in real life.

Just so with regulators: The fear of *corporate* monopoly is used to exaggerate, distort, and over-inflate *government* monopoly. But these things are *ultimately* the same. You need to understand this if you are going to wend your way through the AI future successfully—both as a citizen and as an economic actor—paddling your own canoe through the rapids: *A lot of the future of AI will be about the private and public regulation of data.* The stakes are fun.

Will AI giants convince people that government monopolies are the risk, or vice versa? Will we be stuck careening from extremes, like the fighter jets careening between the Golden Gate and Bay Bridges outside my window (in this "now"), looping around in a cascade of publicly felt G force? How nauseating will that be for citizens, the victims of our own extreme unction? Or will common sense, a balancing prevail? AI is not going to solve this at all. It's going to *exacerbate* whatever we do/decide, for good or ill.

WRONG TERMS AND "U"-TURNS

To be clear, we allow and encourage certain monopolies: over land, over intellectual property (things called patents, copyrights over books, songs, sound recordings, etc.), and, as noted above, over force. A government has a legitimate duty to protect its citizens from internally or externally generated harm.

But every monopoly power—regardless of its source—must be counterbalanced. The social value of a right is in part determined by its limit, or an accompanying duty. All the legal monopolies we are talking about allegedly/typically/ostensibly have checks, balances, or limits associated with them. Patents have limits in time and scope. They are "limited monopolies." Land rights are circumscribed by geophysical boundaries. Government rights are, allegedly, subject to the will of the people governed thereby . . . ultimately.

You can only come on my land if I agree to it. I / you / (the owner in question) has the *right to exclude.* I have the right to limit access within my little tract of monopoly—as long as I don't try to stop traffic on a nearby highway, shoot past the fence, etc.

But humans are sneaky, and we are always trying to parlay one land grant into another and greater one: *President for life! It's an emergency, people! Special corporate voting shares! Patent families! I own that river! I own that vote! They stole that election! Those* [insert external threat here, real or exaggerated] *means we have to "cut some corners" (out of your rights / property / life / ethnic or religious group) for the greater good.*

And what about data?!! *Who owns that river?* Can we really have a data monopoly, like any other kind of legal monopoly? Not super clear, but we think not; not exactly in the grand sense of things.

The amount of new data being created by the world is exponentially increasing. It's always changing. One can always create or find some new data in the exploding flower of the Internet of Things and the billions of connected humans connecting with tens and tens of billions of devices and digital artifacts and automatons talking among themselves. The key is speed. How *long* does it take to create new data reservoirs, clean water / curated data, and where are they?

In the United States, there is plenty of water. But it is disproportionately "allocated" to the Eastern part of the country. The "West" is relatively dry. It takes time and resources to get water from (or in) one place instead of another. We in California see that all the time. Even the north is relatively water-rich compared to the hotter south, and the agrarian central valley is constantly in a state . . . of California and of agitation . . . to get more water. Forest fires abound.

Just so with data.

By having large chunks of data, plus superior algorithms, plus superior technological networks and distribution systems, plus great product-solution features, one company can get a huge lead over others such that it has a simulated, or temporary "data monopoly." Such a company can grow profits and better AI before another can catch up with it. The compounding effect of that "data flywheel" accelerates them past new entrants into the market.

Remember, more than farms or airplanes or toys: Software, and particularly AI-based big data systems, become vastly more efficient with scale. They become more profitable, yes, but they also get more efficient with scale. As one Silicon Valley entrepreneur said, "Intelligence is compounding."

"Artificial intelligence," in turn, is automatically compounding (or automatically "stupiding," depending on your data set). What if they are so good, net net, that consumers are drawn to them inevitably? Is it the giant's fault for being so "beautiful," so to speak? Or is our case a little more complicated?

So what if a big giant captures a huge portion of your a) creativity, b) data, and c) focus? What of the same for a large portion of humanity? Will the Hubris of the Valley save us from Washington overregulation, or backfire? I do not know the answer, but I've read a lot of Greek myths.

In California's central valley, at just the right time, the walnut trees all bloom simultaneously. Have you ever seen an ocean, people? It's just like that, but made up of white flowers. It lasts a brief period, and then they are gone. An ocean of white to an ocean of just plain trees again. This is large-scale industry at its most beautiful. It requires a vast amount of water to create this phenomenon. We can appreciate the beauty, but also understand the need for balanced control of resources.

As with water, so too with data. The "flower" of AI can be spectacularly beautiful, from a mathematical perspective. Those production capabilities can deliver vast new utilities to consumers, as far as the eye of the economy can see. The challenge lies in not veering too far to the extremes, and not falling so in love with the beauty that we forget to nourish the remainder of our state.

COMPLIANCE, PROGRESS, ARTS FINANCIAL

I cannot say that the "most legally compliant" companies are the most commercially successful. I wish I could. But I cannot. It's not a one-to-one correspondence. You need chutzpah and appropriate sales, operational skill, user empathy, human and financial resources, and many other things to build a successful business. It's not *just* legal, by a long shot. (So be legally disciplined, but not crazily so. Don't fixate in a way that kills off your commercial "oomph.")

What I *can* say is that good legal *ab initio* ("from the beginning," in Latin) will help you *keep* the money and the business you make. Nonexistent, sloppy, or bad legal compliance will definitively put your hard-won commercial progress at risk. First, someone, even a trusted partner you've known for a long time (and certainly other folks), may steal your stuff—your money, or even your entire business. Second, if you "steal" from *others*, a) you are doing something bad (karma, people), and b) your stuff is *definitely* going to be at risk, whether immediately or in the future, when those people figure out what happened.

But, really, if all you care about is money, this is really not the book for you. We are happy with capitalism, thank you. It does some good. But it has to be leavened with morality . . . and for morality to have any power, it has to be embodied in law. (This is why AI giants talking "AI ethics" is a red herring.) And for law to have any immediate structuring power in your business, it has to be embodied in your policies, in the way you do business, and in the way that you treat people.

You can make this argument from an atheistic perspective, or you can make it from a religious one: Don't be so greedy that you hurt people. 'Nuff said on that generally. *Specifically?* We're just beginning. In AI, we call the specific applications of "Don't be so greedy you hurt people" Data Control. It applies to how you should act as a consumer or user of AI / big data systems, and it applies to the way you build your own AI. This is the AI adage: *Don't be so greedy for data (or intellectual property) that you hurt people. Users first. Profits as a dependent function of user happiness and value.*

DATA CONTROL IN PRACTICE

As we said in chapter 1, Garbage in, garbage out. Conversely: Gold in, gold out. Correction, for AI: Garbage in, an infinitude of garbage out. Remember: The advantage of advanced software platforms is that they scale. If the system completes "X" task correctly for "Y" person, it can generally do that 100X or a million times (again, assuming task and output similarities). But, same with *in*correct outputs.

See the example of Tay in chapter 1. We could have expected that teenagers would be teenagers (not to excuse any bigotry, but kids do stupid stuff sometimes . . . duh). We should have monitored the intake, even for a REALLY COOL NERD EXPERIMENT! More so, we need to prep for bad actors, Neo-Nazis, criminals, mafia, etc. We need to *design with the bad end in mind, in order to avoid it.* Nerds are not historically so awesome at this. See . . . the Internet.

However, even if you get some weird data in the system (bad apples or bad "applets"), you can correct messy percepts. For example, AI systems can take bad pictures and spotty audio and algorithmically "correct" them—within a certain degree of user defined accuracy—so that they look or sound "normal." (And here I actually mean, generally, "normal" in the statistical sense. You can't correct a picture of an aberrant reality with a statistically normalizing AI.) Bad content can also be handled, to some extent, as long as it is *common* bad content. Bad words can get blocked. Ditto Nazi flags, etc. (or any bigoted flag). But bad guys get creative. They use code words. They use benign language to camouflage malicious intent. This is a trickier content feed problem. The solution? Combine identity verification with content monitoring technology. Don't give unknown people live feeds to billions of users. Qualify 'em.

Besides the data intake distortion problem, here is the other super-duper common problem in building AI: Data rights . . . or, more particularly, the absence thereof.

To build the best AI in the world (and the West Coast of America does—in this instant of the long now), we have taken unlimited liberties with the data of others. China's government even more so. In fact, many countries take liberties with its citizens' data that would confound American constitutional rights. They can potentially build some of the most powerful facial recognition in the world, with unlimited access to identity card and street camera data, at least for their "corpus" of people. However, civil liberties? *Nyet.*

What to do as one concerned with both AI utility and human rights? And the dilemma doesn't end with governments.

We have "click-through" terms of use agreements that provide unfettered access and usage of consumer data for any and all and an infinitude of AI's commercial purposes—*corporate purposes*, enabled by AI. It is like Native Americans trading territory for glass beads. There is no concept of "data rights" so we dispense with them *ab initio.*

Now, we are in the midst of a massive backlash against such contracts, both in Europe, California, and elsewhere. The law requires much stricter and less-exploitive treatment of consumer data, particularly personal data.

Another favorite tactic of every start-up ever (and of some nefarious academics) is to "scrape" data from other people's websites (and by "people," I mean people, but mostly companies). This is almost always a breach of the terms of use agreements of such websites. There are free and open sources of AI useful data out there. Try to use them. Theft is bad karma. Often, it is illegal too.

Intake, usage, and data rights: There are *three* horns to the AI creation dilemma. What are *you* going to do? Here are some heuristics.

Data Control Principles

1. **Don't steal.** *Make sure the data you are using is yours, or that you have clean rights to it.* Even if you have legal agreements (like "terms of use" click-throughs on a website) that give you certain rights, try to anticipate the potential blowback when your consumers/clients figure out that you may have overreached.
2. **Tell the truth** (to the AI you are developing). *Make sure your base data is "accurate" as you understand it.* Don't make a Tay; make an ***An*-**TAY. (Happiness is a warm pun.) Don't use garbage inputs, or data that contains a lot of "false," biased, or incorrect tags. Remember: These AIs are like kids. Don't tell them false, racist, or biased stuff. Be a good parent / uncle / fellow business denizen.
3. **Control, control, control.** In other words: *Control in three ways. First, control the inputs (see above). Then lock down and protect your data sets while they are running through the AI factory. This is like factory security and quality control. Third, control carefully what data / AI factory outputs the end user sees and consumes.*

In yet other words, you have to build a complete data control system, from end to end, that evolves with the platform.

In summary: *Build a system for governing inputs, outputs, and outlets.* Make sure that the entire data cycle for your AI platform is controlled, from soup to nuts, from precipitation to river delta. *Manage the data to manage the AI.* Give as much attention to your data and data systems as to your algorithms and technology applications themselves. That also, and particularly, means *training* your people well, to effectuate compliance.

What does this look like? We are going to see these axioms / common senses (plural!) applied in chapter 6, to both of our cases.

COMMONSENSE AI

I suppose you could say that a lot of the above data control stuff is "common sense." But as we know, *AI does not have common sense.* Nor do most nerds.

In other words, common sense is . . . *not.* It is actually rare, especially where opaque technology, mathematics, and big words are involved. You have to impose the common sense, actively! You have to have a plan and actively carve away the list of foibles and hubrises and crimes you know are bound to arise in *any* big data or AI development project. *You know all the dumb stuff that the smartest nerds—and their automatic minions—are going to do if you don't manage them. Actively!* The magnitude of a nerd brain is often inversely correlated to the magnitude of the commonsense brain. Smart–Dumb. Simple–Smart. No one is perfect. And it is not because anyone is *bad* because they want to create AI. There is just a naiveté in technically driven creation. We do not expect our wonderful creation to be used for ill. It takes objective—and active—common sense to see the way forward, to write the "program" for handling the program.

Again, we have to be explicit about rules for data; rather, *you* need to be explicit about rules and treatment of data. Because if you don't, we can expect chaos . . . chaos self-learning chaos at the speed of artificial intelligence. Like an airplane that creates new airplanes that constantly fly in chaotic directions.

In "air traffic control" and our technological evolution, we need Blue Angels—not Blue Meanies.

6

EDEN CASE STUDIES

So, let's put all of EDEN together and apply its elements to a couple of real-life scenarios or platforms.

Our first example, Lex Machina, deals with a software system we built at Stanford University from about 2006 to 2009 to track US lawsuits and their outcomes (initially, intellectual property cases). The analogy is too strong, but think of it as a kind of "Moneyball" for federal lawsuits. The system is still in massive use today. Like the airplane that gets faster and better with use, the more lawsuit data types and event data that's fed into it, the more curation and quality control done by experts, the better the system gets. Lex Machina exhibits network effects.

Why can I talk about this application? Lex Machina was "opensourced" when it was spun out of Stanford. This means that our basic methods at the time—which my comments are strictly limited to—are shareable with you. We have also shared certain basic details over the years, because of our public service–oriented mandate. The second use case I can talk about because it was originally a white paper for a governmental body, bound by statute to share certain data with the public and its monitoring agencies and groups.

In contrast to the above software platform, our next example, "FinCity," is fictional; it bears no relation to any actual project at time of writing. It arose as a thought experiment from a real-life need.

In October of 2018, I got a call that led to my appointment as a special advisor to the United Kingdom's Financial Conduct Authority (FCA). The FCA is one of the primary financial, insurance, and securities regulators in the UK, and thus impacts quite a bit of commerce worldwide. They were looking to automate some of their rules compliance mechanisms, including automating the logic code to execute their rule book on how much money banks had to keep on their books, and other stuff.

My question was: Why not write the rules as software code to begin with? Better yet, since we were creating a data model for the entire system, why not deploy AI platforms to test and improve the FCA's ability to support financial system users/participants and institutional aims? What data and software frameworks would we need to support FCA goals, in an ideal world?

LEX MACHINA EDEN APPLICATION

Once upon a time, the US federal judiciary had a very limited understanding of its own intellectual property lawsuits: How many (to some extent), what types, what the outcomes were, and how those outcomes ended up being the end.

This is a bit like being a factory owner and not knowing:

1. Output: how many widgets you are making every day, and of what subtypes;
2. Raw materials: how much a) you needed, and b) was actually going into the factory;
3. Quality: of anything—widgets, raw materials, suppliers, workers, managers, etc.;
4. Price versus net cost: whether anyone was buying your widgets, whether they were even the right widget at all, whether any particular widget was actually worth producing.

In other words, whether any stratum of production is "successful."

The pain of this "unknowing" was pretty large, and so a professor at Stanford Law School decided to do something about it. He conceived of a database that would cover all intellectual property cases. He raised millions of dollars to put the project together (mostly from donations from different kinds of big companies), and got ready to go.

But there was a problem.

A judicial system is generally a lot more complicated than a factory, and way less predictable. (For example: The parties to a lawsuit are "fighting" each other.) Nor did "factories" for dealing with legal text then exist. They *especially* didn't exist for that scale and complexity of text. The deeper you go into a case, the more complex and nuanced it generally gets. The project was arguably doomed.

Solution? One person (me) crazy enough to try and architect and build the sucker and a bunch of AI (suffering through a lot of "no's" to bring in two of the top AI talents in machine learning and natural language processing to the project). As you can probably predict at this point in the book, the "AI" started with a heck of a lot of "I": Read, some dude sitting in a basement (yep, same dude as above), tagging thousands of documents as X/Y/Z/"Orangutan"/ etc., then working with engineers to automate such analytic "sweat."

But, blood, sweat, and tears aside, let's see how our analytical framework, EDEN, helps us build a successful project (which happens to involve some stuff people call "artificial intelligence").

Lex-Empirical. The primary empirical data ecosystem comprised the "states" and outcomes of federal patent litigation, as expressed in legal documents and docket entry codes (specialized speech or "metadata" that each case and case event was tagged with).

Lex-Design. In the Lex Machina platform, the primary users were: judges; attorneys (at a) law firms and b) companies); and regular citizens. There were a bunch of other types, too (press, academics, non-lawyer governmental, etc.), but the preceding three were probably the biggies. (Ultimately, the ultimate user was an insurance company. But that's a detail for a later time.)

Lex-Evolution. Evolution came in two parts:

1. First, we constantly worked to improve the a) accuracy and b) scope of our legal event classification systems (constantly reintroducing expert user feedback—e.g., from judges and judges' clerks—into both of those evolutionary pathways); and

2. We constantly worked to expand, reapply, and then sell our legal classification systems to new types of lawsuits (i.e., from patent to copyright, antitrust, trademark, and eventually securities law, etc.). This allowed us to a) build once but b) sell many times, the exact same AI function. This latter feature is the fundamental benefit of advanced software.

Lex-Net. We "netted" complex AI outputs by weighing multiple things in the court dockets for relevant cases, including both the text that found within legal documents and the text that described those documents. We also included a set of complex human tags (done by us) in trying to constantly perfect our classification or legal event and outcome tagging system. Just determining what kind of document a legal document was (i.e., any single document attached to a case) involved dozens of different data types that we needed to correlate in order to get an accurate result to the user. We also "netted" the AI output data in the sense that we synthesized and presented national patent litigation and other court data to all three branches of the US federal government.

FINCITY EDEN APPLICATION

Once upon a time, there was a magical lending device called "LI-BOR." LIBOR (short for the London Interbank Offered Rate) was the price/interest rate at which banks would—theoretically—

lend money to each other. If banks lent to each other at X percent interest, you could borrow at the rate of X+Y percent, for everything from housing loans to credit cards.

But there was a problem.

Within and beyond the kingdom, a group of scallywags (individuals) at different banks decided that they could—by communicating improperly—distort the true, virginal beauty of the LIBOR, to their own profit. Their scheme worked, for a time, until they were discovered and banished from the castle.

Amid the ruins of the broken mechanism, the people cried out for justice and reform, and the political gentry heard them. They created a new monitor, a "sheriff," if you will, called the Financial Conduct Authority (FCA). The FCA was charged with policing (and/or perhaps replacing) LIBOR, ensuring the justness and efficacy of the system overall, and generally sweeping and purging the castle and kingdom of all scallywags. (*Sweep and Purge* might be a great title for a novel, but it is *not*, to my knowledge, the name of a bar in San Francisco.)

However, as in a city after a great fire, the grounds and streets can be rebuilt anew—more streamlined, more functional, and perhaps even more beautiful.

In furtherance of its goal to protect financial consumers and help optimize system health in general, the FCA was also specifically charged with:

a. being reasonably efficient (e.g., in terms of resources spent by itself and third parties); and

b. adapting and adopting beneficial business and technological innovations—as provably practical, reliable, and economical.

In other words, our knight errant commissioned new armor, and a new steed. He further looked for magical artifacts to further his mission.

And so, as they began creating their new regime, the regulatory gentry and the FCA in general realized that they could try new things and be more efficient, not simply reduce the scallywag population to within tolerable limits. They realized that a lot of the way banks reported assets, complied with rules, and shared documents with regulators was redundant or inefficient. There might also be new, more-subtle, and less-expensive means of scallywag detection and deterrence.

In October of 2018, the FCA contacted me (along with numerous others) about trying to further build this new regime efficiently by implementing user software code, user-oriented design, and even AI.

This is what I found.

FinCity Design. In the FinCity platform, the immediate users are financial system regulators. They need to discover problems and measure the health of a very complex, very active, and very, very big financial system. You'll notice that this user is a little more defined than the user set in Lex Machina (for various reasons that I will explain later). It's one type of user, with a general level of sophistication in the space, as opposed to everyone from "super-experts" (like judges) to citizens, for Lex Machina.

Usually it's hard to make a system accessible to both super-experts, on the one hand, and new users without a lot of background, on the other. However, there are ways of doing this in a single, unified system, depending on the use case. (More on this later.)

FinCity-Empirical. But—while FinCity has a simpler user set, the empirical data environment—and, to some extent, the number and diversity of needs/problems of that single user set— are a lot more complicated.

Note that if your user group is super complicated, you probably want to focus on data and events that are pretty simple, and vice versa. If your empirical data environment is super complicated, you probably want to focus on a pretty narrowly tailored user group. As most start-ups know, doing too much, for too many people, is a recipe for failure. This is all the more true of a single AI platform developer or manager—which you may be. In a word: *Focus.*

FinCity's empirical data set is comprised of financial holdings (e.g., money, and data about where bits of money sit), transactions (e.g., the legal text of agreements and the commercial execution thereof, as embodied in data), and legal entities or persons involved in those transactions (including regular consumers, but also banks and myriad other specific legal entities). Those data are our ecosystem.

We can also gather and include similar or analogous classes of data from other financial regulatory systems—like those from American or Asian financial systems—but this, again, is a secondary consideration.

FinCity-Net. We are going to "net" various transaction and entity monitoring systems by measuring data flows and holdings of money and financial instruments across time. Anomalous events (e.g., fraud in the system, undue pricing power for any single entity, a consumer "crash" or extreme negative loss) are all "netted" from our myriad data inputs, which the banks and others are required to send to us (i.e., our financial regulatory "user").

FinCity Evolution. This is a doozy for FinCity. Here, I argue that the "evolution" we are looking for in the system is not just in our AI platform. Sure, we can and should get better and better at detecting and preventing financial fraud, antitrust violations, and other anomalies in the UK's financial system. That is part and parcel of what we do, and we do it by constantly "red teaming" (or having outside bodies "test" and challenge the system outputs through sampling and traditional audit and analysis methods) the AI platform, and incorporating such learnings into the next system release.

In addition, we will use such methods to identify and prevent entirely novel types of fraud and bad actors—much like big companies hire teams of "hackers" to test their systems (try to break in without really breaking in or stealing anything), or like defense departments test their own national defense measures. (More on this later.)

But we are going to define a more-explicit evolutionary measure for this use case: *We define the evolutionary goal as improving the financial system itself, overall.* First and foremost: We define system goals / utility for the UK and other participants/regulatees. From governmental utility, we derive ways we can improve the software system in support of such broader societal (and regulatory-stature) goals.

By extending and "mirroring" AI system utility to societal or client group utility (e.g., AI system functionality matches, mirrors, or reflects financial system utility), we can start helping societies at scale—or, at the least, large and significant client groups.

DATA CONTROL APPLIED TO CASES

This subsection runs data control through our same use cases.

Lex Machina Data Control

There were four major elements to our data control plan for this project:

1. compliant crawlers for raw data;
2. human/team training;
3. legal protocols; and
4. technical protection measures.

For Lex Machina, we didn't scrape the federal district court websites, which is the first instinct of a lot of small or new companies. We painstakingly built nearly one hundred unique web crawlers that acted precisely as a human, clicking all the right buttons to ensure that we a) complied with their terms of use, as they allowed bots that precisely mimicked what human users would do; and b) paid for every bit of data we were supposed to pay for. For the search data, what data users searched for, we put the fear of G-d into our people.

If a bad (or sloppy) actor inside the company had looked at, say, judicial clerk search records, and mouthed off about them to their lawyer or other friends, it could expose the judicial process to inappropriate scrutiny. I not only told my team that this (or even the equivalent for law firm searches) would completely destroy the company; I also told them there could be extraordinarily severe—and potentially federal—legal consequences for such a bad actor.

Maybe I was just a tad strong, but we had no incidents whatsoever of that sort on my watch (and to my knowledge, the company never did either). Building those unique crawlers was a huge pain, but I noticed that along the way, we passed the wreckage of many other companies that used mass crawlers or some other weird, noncompliant, or stochastic (i.e., randomly determined) method of data gathering. Those companies did not survive.

Our way was just one way, but the key was that it was 100 percent legal and scalable, with the right resources. We had one incident where an academic tried to download all the data in our entire system, right before the Thanksgiving holiday. This was detected (albeit, a bit late), and we remedied the situation (think: calling university counsel, verifying that all data was deleted).

After that, we implemented technical measures so that no one user could download a material portion of our data (no one regular user would ever need to anyway). This is known as "data throttling," and is a common method of data protection, even from "authorized users."

Another technical measure is checking user location, which can be a heuristic for security risk. (There are all kinds of ways around traceroute user location on the Internet, so it isn't usable in all cases. But, as with AI outputs, security is a "net" situation where we are compiling and using many different features to improve outcome.)

Lastly, the thing that allowed us to 1) successfully "undo" (delete the corpus) of the overzealous data-downloading professor; and 2) ensure that our employees maintained the strictest levels of secrecy for user data was that we had good agreements: a) a user-access agreement that gave the user reasonable rights but limited what they could take, so as not to harm the company or the whole of the project; and b) agreements with our employees (and any contractors), so that they had a legal duty to protect user secrecy, not just a job imperative. (On the former, the one I wrote stayed in use for at least ten years after I wrote it. Awesome!)

Again, there are four legs to the data control stool: 1) compliant crawlers/intake; 2) rock-solid legal protocols (employee and user / third party); 3) technical measures (security *plus* data throttling *plus* being alert to anomalies); and, most importantly, 4) team training. You have to tell your teams *why* this stuff is important, and explain the risks of sloppy or nonexistent data control.

FinCity Data Control

For FinCity (and again, this is a theoretical platform), we are developing systems for the government itself. This is dangerous. The government is so powerful that it needs to restrain itself so as not to be too heavy-handed, especially given the sensitivities UK Parliament baked into the Financial Conduct Authority when it was created. It was designed to be responsive to consumers foremost, of course, but also to industry, and was charged with close attention to the balance between its regulatory outputs/asks and the burdens such asks imposed on the "regulatees." Efficiency.

So! *One*: Create a detailed *data intake and usage protocol* which spells out 1) the data classes the FCA gets, and from whom for each such class (including not just banks and insurance companies, but also consumers, whistleblowers, and people who complain, etc.; these classes should be specific, but flexible enough to evolve); and 2) how each of those data classes may be a) *used*; and, equally importantly, b) *not used*.

Two: Create a plan to pull in exogenous ("outside") sets of data, to augment what it is getting directly from financial entities, trades, consumers, etc. For example, the FCA might find weird or interesting economic data from other countries, the EU, or even from third parties in the UK itself to augment its core data sets. It should be extremely careful about how it pairs and combines exogenous data with core data, both in terms of reliance and in terms of potential insights. It should treat third-party data with skepticism, but be open to using it for anomaly or crime/violation detection. For example, if it finds an unusual or unexpected result, it may be appropriate to report it, but not necessarily as "truth" unless such outside data is verified carefully. As with health and nutrition, the government should not give its weight to untested hypotheses. But it *can* continue to ask hard questions about its recommendations and approaches.

Three: Establish equally specific standards (not necessarily straitjacketed rules) about data reporting and access to analytic output for: 1) its oversight committees; 2) internal experts (not everyone in the FCA gets *everything* / data throttling); 3) industry; 4) professionals; and 5) the public. Ideally, the FCA produces a *dashboard* on activity and on financial industry health generally. Such a dashboard may have *tailored views* for different types of users.

Four: Every hacker in the world is going to try and get inside the FCA. Between the aggregated banking and holdings data, plus the strategic economic data, the FCA will need protection (training and hard-core IT) from the top of the top UK security specialists. It needs to treat security as a living, dynamic process that is never finished. It can rely on physical locale to help geo-fence certain types of sensitive data. The hard part is doing this without making it onerous to FCA employees and affiliates. There is a lot more to creating a data control plan for an entity—a truly complex and important endeavor—but a good start includes: 1) a data intake and usage protocol, 2) an exogenous data integration system, 3) a data access protocol and supporting technologies (especially for "finished" analytics), and 4) a live / constantly evolving security and training regimen.

How would you pay for a strong version of the above FCA data control protocol?

One must begin with a utility calculation of the entire FCA system, then price out what is attributable to the above (including avoiding breaches / criminal exploitation), and then do what one can. Some of this (training, people) can be done surprisingly cheaply. Other things, like analytics dashboards, can be bought using "off the shelf" software components/licenses, then customizing them. Make do, but *do* do.

As you can see above, the FCA has already supplemented (or will need to further supplement) its cybersecurity efforts, most likely with outside experts. This is a general issue in AI / "big data" platforms: use of outside experts. You have the ability to resolve a lot of nontechnical issues yourself, but it's okay (and sometimes preferable) to tap outside experts on things like security and the law. However, even to manage IT security experts and lawyers, you have to learn enough to ensure that these folks won't take undue liberties with your projects, resources, time, and/or money. You need to at least learn enough about data rights and security that you can ask these outside experts good questions, and manage them.

THE POLITICS OF AI

Remember, as we established before, "AI" is presently as much a marketing meme as a real technology. Don't add to the fuss. Just so, today, at this interval of time, many "AI" business projects are for show. They are "innovation theater"—designed to maximize market credit for being techy without the hard, brutal, data-bound reality that real process improvements inevitably require. The grit of the data is required for traction, and most people don't have the personal grit to get through it, to fix what needs to be fixed, to clean what needs to be cleaned, to legal-schematize everything, to be disciplined in all the areas required for a good AI project. Right now, people just want the credit. And that desire for an easy win in AI is the key to project failure. To wit: *Pretension is the thief of action.*

Eventually, the number of real AI projects, that do real work, is going to exceed the number of plays at your company's "innovation theater." Technological "show ponies" will be replaced with advanced AI horsepower, applied for practical, reasonable ends.

At least do your best to make sure that your AI project is *Masterpiece Theatre*, and not just a lame puppet show. Better yet, get something *done*.

Here are some suggestions for maximizing that probability.

First, name your project after what it is designed to do. Don't use "AI" in the name at all, unless you really need it for funding (or marketing). For example, give it a name that symbolizes or reflects what the platform is going to *do*: Eggplant Classifier, Rutabaga Sorter, Ice-Cream Maker, Mother-in-Law Evasion System, etc. The AI should be under the surface so the user isn't even aware of it. It should be like magic, as modern search engines don't show you any part of how they get their seemingly miraculous search results to you.

Second, don't use the word *disruption* unless you really have to (or unless you are a start-up and the only people you are ostensibly "disrupting" are direct competitors). Being a "disrupter" of existing company business lines sounds really awesome unless a) you actually work for a big company (which most of you do), or b) you are not the CEO and control 100 percent of the board. Why? The people you are disrupting may kill your project (and/or your job prospects). By definition, they are running a "big business" with, potentially, lots of revenue which, yes, means clout. You don't want to alienate all the people in your company with clout before you even start your project. Name it "Business Line X Accelerant"! Catalyze your folks' business lines.

Don't make the people you need to carry out and effectuate actual innovation feel like dinosaurs. Empower them. They will support you for it down the road. Odds are, a good chunk of them *know* their business line or product may need to evolve (including with or via AI analytics). They just don't want to be crushed underfoot. Empower them. Train them. Teach them what you know. *Share this book with them.* Don't patronize. You see what trouble Silicon Valley creates, needlessly, by effectuating nerdery with hubris.

There's another reason you should avoid alienating the Old Guard (in addition to them having power over your project and career). Remember our little discussions about data? You can't automate any process without the help of policy experts in the relevant analytic task. You need their wisdom and experience to get a good data corpus, or at least to define what success looks like when it's effectuated through the sales process. Every AI platform is unique. If yours is dumb because you alienated all the people who could make it smart, because you wanted to be a "cool disrupter" and show off to your CEO before you've actually done anything . . . well. I'm not going to say "Shame on you," but we'd rather you be successful than pretentious.

BACK TO THE BAR

Here's a little story. In 2018 I was named to a committee of the California State Bar that was looking at using AI and automation to expand access to justice and legal rights. What could be better, right?

Well . . .

The committee merely recommended that the Bar "explore" the highly regulated (!!) provision of some services via software (without the direct intervention of a licensed attorney at every second) and . . . well, from the reaction, you would have thought the zombie Armageddon was nigh!

There were lots of great critiques of some of the committee's suggestions. Heck, I didn't agree with them all, and was on record as being on the conservative end of the committee, to ensure that attorneys (the "incumbents," potential "disruptees") were always in the driver's seat on legal automation.

But what we got from a lot of critics wasn't reasoned concern. Not pointed questions, but medieval fear-mongering. People were going to die if we let software help people! Amazon would take over the legal profession. The world would end. There would be no more legal jobs.

Let me tell you something: Amazon doesn't *need* a legal change to change or have an influence on the legal profession. It already has a world-class distribution platform. It (or other parties) will have an influence regardless of the state of the law, and assuming its perfect compliance with existing law.

The parties that radically need a change in the law are . . . lawyers! Attorneys can't get funding—not like start-ups, or companies that can raise capital. Not, generally, at time of writing, in the United States. *That* is why attorney jobs are disappearing. We have been hiding our heads in the sand, avoiding process innovation and technology, for, say, two hundred years? Longer? People are dying *now*, people are radically underserved, because attorneys have failed to effectively engage with quantitative data, or any profession other than their own, and are as arrogant in their tower as the most radical nerds in the most self-contained server room / computer science artifice. *Arrogance* kills innovation, and so does fear.

You will need to learn to manage the "fear of the long tail," the "middle market," and "the middle managers" in any AI project. My advice: Speaking from long and painful experience: 1) Demystify the AI (use this book and break it down); and 2) Teach the new through the old, as Aristotle said. For Lex Machina, we didn't talk about selling data to anyone. (No one knew what that meant for court stuff at the time.) We sold them "history," and that's all that data is.

Those nerds (and AI project managers) who do not know their AI (and data) history are doomed to repeat it, in an endless loop. You have been given a gift—the ability to learn from the mistakes of others, the "best and brightest mistakes," the mistakes that have burned holes through society, like cigarette embers through a down blanket.

You have the gift of creating a new future for yourself that your AI cannot see. Your AI merely magnifies your current vision. Run with it.

It's time.

AFTERWORD: MIND THE GAP

Ethics and AI

Joshua Schulz, PhD, Professor of Philosophy,
DeSales University

WHAT IS ETHICS?

Let's begin with what ethics is not.

Ethics is not the law. Slavery was both legal and immoral. We use ethics to determine which laws are just, not vice versa. Ethics is not determined by culture. That would make ethics vary with geography, while murder is wrong everywhere. Nor do your personal beliefs determine ethics. Beliefs are made true or false by the way the world is—by whether the cat is or is not on the mat—and ethical beliefs are no different. You just have to know which parts of reality to look at.

Ethics *is* rational, reflective, and creative—everything that distinguishes you from a machine. Ethics is *rational* because it involves thinking carefully about how the world is, about what kind of person you want to be, and how people flourish together in society. Ethics is *reflective* because it forces us to question social expectations about the roles we occupy. The "I was just doing my job" defense of Adolf Eichmann, one of the main organizers of the

Holocaust, does not work for tasks that are immoral in the first place. And ethics is *creative* because it is a form of problem-solving. No abstract rule can tell you how to behave in every situation. You have to decide which ethical ideas are relevant to your situation, and how to apply them in your particular case. A man once spat on Mother Teresa when she begged him for food. She thanked him and asked if he had anything for the starving boy at her side to eat. This saint was a moral artist. What would you have done?

Technology ethics is about minding the gaps—two of them, to be exact.

First, there is a gap between material and moral progress. Having technological conveniences does not always improve our lives. Modern agriculture fills our grocery stores with cheap food but imposes costs on our environment. Smartphones put the Internet in our pockets, but how many people waste time on them at work, or struggle with addictions to gaming, social media, or pornography, to the detriment of their family, friends, and loved ones? Power without wisdom can make for a dangerous fool.

Second, there is a gap between technological power and the common good. Our moral learning curve is arithmetic, while technological power grows exponentially. Cambridge Analytica was able to manipulate an American presidential election using data analytics and social media because law responds to harm but does not always anticipate it. Millions of people signed up for Facebook, Twitter, and Snapchat accounts before we realized social media can make us lose friends and alienate people.

You stand in those gaps—not politicians, police, or churchmen. Minding the gaps is *your* responsibility as a citizen and as a human being. Mere compliance with the law will not guarantee that you have acted ethically, and in the digital age, your stakeholders will call out your ethical failures before the law does anyway. No rule or moral guru can tell you what to do in every situation. You need to think independently, creatively, and responsibly, both to protect yourself and others, and, more importantly, to live a life you and your children can be proud of, to build a better future for us all.

DOING GOOD AND AVOIDING EVIL

Beware of complex ethical theories. The basic ideas of ethics are commonsensical.

First, all human beings have a kind of value we call *dignity*. We can *wrong* them. Respecting people's dignity means treating them with justice, as persons rather than things or resources. It means respecting their knowledge, preferences, and desire to determine the course of their own lives. We are not born to be slaves.

Second, all human beings are living bodies. We can *harm* them. Bodies are dependent, needy things which grow, mature, decline, are differently abled or disabled, and so on. Respecting people's bodies means *caring* for them in all of their vulnerability, in all of their physical uniqueness. It means avoiding biases and thinking creatively about how we can help physically diverse people become full participants in the digital age.

Third, we are social and political beings. The English poet John Donne once wrote that, "No man is an island entire of itself; every man is a piece of the continent, a part of the main; . . . any man's death diminishes me, because I am involved in mankind." This fact is ever more apparent in a globalized, networked world. The flourishing of our families depends on the well-being of our communities, and the well-being of our communities depends on the health of our political life together. The Judeo-Christian tradition, to which I belong, calls this caring for the *common good*, counseling us to make sure that how we act as a group, as a body politic, is just and caring for the *whole*. It also proposes a measure of our success: How capable of flourishing, with the help of our community, are the worst off among us? Do our social and political institutions, including our technological culture, frustrate or facilitate our well-being?

Let's be frank: The modern world is dignity-poor, benevolence-poor, and justice-poor—not always because we are malicious, but more often because we are too negligent or too busy to care.

Mind the gaps. Be ethically proactive. Be your brother's (and sister's) keeper.

ETHICS AND AI

Applied AI involves special challenges calling for your creativity and courage. A few are listed below, because, as technology ethicist Shannon Vallor says, ethics is like birdwatching. Like birds, ethical issues are everywhere, but they are easy to miss or ignore, and learning to recognize them is a skill that takes effort to get right. It also gets easier with practice. Following each challenge are suggested questions that will help you begin thinking about the ethics of your project. They are not exhaustive, so by all means, add some of your own.

The Master–Slave Dilemma

The nineteenth-century German philosopher Georg Wilhelm Friedrich Hegel said a stupid slave is useless, but smart slaves threaten to become our masters. He was talking about technology! The more powerful our tools are, the more convenient they become. The more we rely on technology, the easier it is to deny that we are responsible for its negative effects. Remember that machines work for *us*, and we are on the hook for whatever good or evil they do. Automated systems intensify this dilemma.

Relevant Questions

- How can we ensure that our technology supports human judgment rather than replaces it?
- How can we retain effective control and ethical oversight over our machines?
- How can we avoid turning algorithms into inscrutable, black-box masters of our actions?

- How can we ensure that users have enough information to make informed choices about their use of our technology, or its impact on their lives?
- What does accountability look like during the design, rollout, and support stages of your project?

"Rappaccini's Daughter"

Nathaniel Hawthorne wrote a tragic story about a girl in medieval Italy who tended a garden of poisonous plants for her father, a doctor and researcher. His daughter developed resistance to them but became poisonous herself. Hawthorne's lesson is that progress is two-sided. Why? Because we are two-sided. Every technology magnifies some element of human nature: our strength (from hammers to industrial robots), our senses (from hearing aids to telescopes), and our mental powers (computers). That's why technology is so useful; we use it to do what we *already* do, *better*. But it also magnifies our dark side, making it easier to act on our greed, anger, and unrestrained impulses. For every positive thing that's been done with a technical tool, you can bet it's been used for something negative. People are going to use your solution for good *and* evil in ways you may not have imagined. Are you prepared for that?

Relevant Questions

- What kinds of incentives do various stakeholders have to use your technology for good and for evil?
- How can you design your tech to incentivize what's good and discourage what's not?
- What are some alternative uses of your tech?
- What is the worst thing someone could do (or have done to them) with your tech? How can you plan for it and mitigate it when it happens?

Epistemological Bias

Those who study epistemology study knowledge—how we know what we think we know. Machines are *calculators*, not *thinkers* or *knowers*. They crunch numbers without understanding what those numbers *mean*. They will not recognize bias based on social or economic class, sex or gender, race or ethnicity, or other factors implicit in your data sets. They will not worry that achieving mathematical efficiency means a certain number of people will go without jobs or health care, or in general, how false positives or false negatives will make innocent people suffer.

Relevant Questions

- Is your data just? That is, is it relevant and representative of all of us, or does it represent an economically and educationally privileged, racially and ethnically narrow, or ideologically siloed set of people?
- How can we ensure that our mistakes avoid harming or punishing the innocent and vulnerable, even if that means less profit and efficiency?

Manipulation and Marginalization

In order to be effective, your AI project will need more data than any single person possesses or can make sense of. This *information asymmetry* is what makes AI so useful. But it also means creating inequalities of power that can be used to infantilize, exploit, and marginalize people. If the poor or disabled cannot access your technology, it builds an invisible wall between them and the opportunities and benefits your technology is supposed to create. If your technology makes decisions for people, it may end up treating them like children rather than adults. And always remember that the sensitive information people share with your tech makes them targets for the unscrupulous. Strive to give every user of your tech a safe, equal opportunity to make decisions that will improve their lives in real and meaningful ways.

Relevant Questions

• Do people give you informed, competent, and free consent to use their data, and are you clear about how you will use, store, and protect that data?
• Are you gathering the relevant minimum data needed for your tech to be effective?
• Does your tech prey on people's ignorance, bad luck, circumstances, or inability to respond when it harms them?
• Are the benefits and harms of your tech equally shared between you, your users, and other stakeholders, or will your tech create inequalities of wealth and opportunity?
• Will your tech benefit the present at the expense of future generations, or the environment?

BEST PRACTICES

Many ethical violations in applied AI are unintentional. They are caused by a lack of attention or imagination, or by old-fashioned ignoring of stakeholder feedback. Happily, this also means that most ethical problems can be avoided or mitigated by performing regular due diligence during the development, testing, and rollout of your technology. In short: Don't save ethics for the afterword! Put it first, right alongside compliance with the law.

To help you think about how to incorporate ethical reflection into your creative process, here are five best practices in applied AI.

1. *Ethics first*: Create opportunities to incorporate ethical reflection into every step of the design process. Schedule brainstorming sessions devoted to anticipating, avoiding, and mitigating ethical challenges. Don't design your tech-

nology first and only think about ethical issues the day before rollout; otherwise, you will risk seeing ethics as an inefficiency rather than an element of good design.

2. *Avoid euphemism*: Language matters. We like to hide our bad decisions behind vague and abstract talk, so *be concrete.* Rather than talking about "users," imagine your family and friends using your tech. Phrases about increasing our "quality of life," seeking "progress" or "greater goods," are meaningless. How *exactly* will your tech benefit people? What are the costs of using your tech rather than something else? Who—or what—will end up paying the costs?

3. *Build effective feedback loops*: Your company will thrive if you promote transparency and trustworthiness at each stage of development. That's because when you make a mistake, the world will let you know so you can correct it. The alternative is to be blindsided by errors you did not even know were there. Seek and invite feedback from stakeholders down to the level of data itself. If your data is siloed and unresponsive to changing circumstances, it's likely already outdated or irrelevant.

4. *Plan for the worst-case scenario*: People will misuse your work and use it in non-ideal situations. Can you make the worst misuses difficult or impossible with smart design? How does your tech perform with partial data? In a major weather crisis? After a power outage?

5. *Culture counts*: In Greece more than 2,300 years ago, Aristotle taught that we become what we repeatedly do. He is still right. Teams that build each other up and encourage ethical questions will be open to constructive criticism because it makes their work that much better. If you encourage respectful debate, accept conscientious challenges, and always defend whistleblowers, you trade some short-term troubles for long-term payoffs. Build a corporate culture where it's easy for people to be good.

FURTHER RESOURCES

The Markkula Center for Applied Ethics at Santa Clara University conducts regular research and workshops about how to incorporate ethics into technology development. Many of their resources are available for free online (see https://www.scu.edu/ethics/focus-areas/technology-ethics/).

Stay up-to-date on emerging ethical challenges with the MIT Technology Review: https://www.technologyreview.com/.

Check out the Council for Big Data, Ethics and Society: http://bdes.dtasociety.net. A partner of the National Science Foundation, this website has an excellent bibliography on current issues in data ethics.

NOTES

INTRODUCTION

1. https://www.humanbrainproject.eu/en/.

I. 7 AI MYTHS, 7 AI RULES

1. J. McCarthy, M. L. Minsky, N. Rochester, and C. E. Shannon, "A Proposal for the Dartmouth Summer Research Project on Artificial Intelligence," August 31, 1955. Last modified April 3, 1996. http://www-formal.stanford.edu/jmc/history/dartmouth/dartmouth.html.

2. According to his best-selling, autobiographical book about AI and great power politics: Kai-Fu Lee, *AI Superpowers: China, Silicon Valley, and the New World Order* (Boston: Houghton Mifflin Harcourt, 2018), ch. 7.

3. See Nick Bostrom, *Superintelligence: Paths, Dangers, Strategies* (Oxford, England: Oxford University Press, 2014).

4. http://norman-ai.mit.edu/.

5. Mariya Yao, "Beyond Backpropagation: Can We Go Deeper than Deep Learning?" *Topbots,* November 9, 2017. https://www.topbots.com/deeper-than-deep-learning-beyond-backpropagation-geoffrey-hinton/.

6. Matthew Herper, "MD Anderson Benches IBM Watson in Setback for Artificial Intelligence in Medicine," *Forbes.com,* February 19,

2017. https://www.forbes.com/sites/matthewherper/2017/02/19/md-anderson-benches-ibm-watson-in-setback-for-artificial-intelligence-in-medicine/#3175068f3774.

2. AI IN PLAIN ENGLISH

1. See World Intellectual Property Organization, *Technology Trends 2019: Artificial Intelligence*. https://www.wipo.int/edocs/pubdocs/en/wipo_pub_1055.pdf. The executive summary can be downloaded from https://www.wipo.int/edocs/pubdocs/en/wipo_pub_1055-exe_summary1.pdf.

2. The best book on AI mathematics is Nick Polson and James Scott, *AIQ* (New York: St. Martin's Press, 2018).

3. See https://www.netflixprize.com/community/topic_1537.html and https://www.netflixprize.com/assets/GrandPrize2009_BPC_BellKor.pdf. The irony is that Netflix never actually used the prize-winning algorithm, supposedly because of the excessive engineering expense involved. It has used other algorithms developed by the prize-winning team. Casey Johnston, "Netflix Never Used Its $1 Million Algorithm Due to Engineering Costs," *Ars Technica*, April 16, 2012, https://www.wired.com/2012/04/netflix-prize-costs/.

4. See Polson and Scott, ch. 2.

5. Public domain image from Wikipedia. https://en.wikipedia.org/wiki/Regression_analysis.

6. See Polson and Scott, ch. 2.

7. $P(H|D) = P(H) * P(D|H) / P(D)$. See Polson and Scott, ch. 3.

8. See Polson and Scott, ch. 4.

9. See Polson and Scott, ch. 5.

10. An excellent book on this topic is Steven Finlay, *Artificial Intelligence and Machine Learning for Business: A No-Nonsense Guide to Data-Driven Technologies* (Relativistic, 2nd ed., 2017).

11. Quoted in Clive Cookson, "Huge Surge in AI Patent Applications in Past 5 Years," *Financial Times*, January 31, 2019.

12. Cathy O'Neil, *Weapons of Math Destruction* (New York: Broadway Books, 2016).

13. Madhumita Murgia, "How to Stop Computers Being Biased: The Bid to Prevent Algorithms Producing Racist, Sexist or Class-Conscious Decisions," *Financial Times*, February 12, 2019.

14. We recommend Andrew Ng's courses on machine learning, available for free through Coursera, the online learning platform that he founded. See https://www.coursera.org/.

15. See interview with Erik Cambria in Kim Davis (ed.), *The Promises and Perils of Modern AI* (DMN, 2018) eBook. https://forms.dmnews. com/whitepapers/usadata/0218/?utm_source=DMNTP04302018& email_hash=BBFC7DC6CF59388D09E7DF83D3FE564F& spMailingID=19474637&spUserID=NTMyMTI1MTM4MTMS1& spJobID=1241853091&spReportId=MTI0MTg1MzA5MQS2. For Erik Cambria's work on teaching computers emotional recognition through using semantics and linguistics, see http://sentic.net/.

3. AI APPLICATIONS IN BUSINESS

1. Esat Dedezade, "Leaders Look to Embrace AI, and High-Growth Companies Are Seeing the Benefits," *Microsoft News Centre Europe*, March 5, 2019. https://news.microsoft.com/europe/features/leaders-look-to-embrace-ai-and-high-growth-companies-are-seeing-the-benefits/.

2. Sam Ransbotham, Philipp Gerbert, Martin Reeves, David Kiron, and Michael Spira, "Artificial Intelligence in Business Gets Real," *MIT Sloan Management Review*, September 17, 2018. https://sloanreview.mit. edu/projects/artificial-intelligence-in-business-gets-real/.

3. Evelyn Cheng, "A.I. Could Spur Global Growth as Much as the Steam Engine Did, Study Shows," *CNBC.com*. Last modified September 5, 2018. https://www.cnbc.com/2018/09/05/artificial-intelligence-ai-could-spur-global-growth-study-shows.html.

4. Stew Magnuson, "DARPA Spending $2 Billion to Advance AI Technologies," *NationalDefenseMagazine.org*. September 7, 2018. http:// www.nationaldefensemagazine.org/articles/2018/9/7/darpa-spending-$2-billion-to-advance-ai-technologies.

5. Kai-Fu Lee, *AI Superpowers: China, Silicon Valley, and the New World Order* (Boston: Houghton Mifflin Harcourt, 2018).

6. OECD, "Private Equity Investment in Artificial Intelligence," OECD Going Digital Policy Note, OECD, Paris, December 2018. http://www.oecd.org/going-digital/ai/private-equity-investment-in-artificial-intelligence.pdf.

7. Raymond Perrault, Yoav Shoham, Erik Brynjolfsson, Jack Clark, John Etchemendy, Barbara Grosz, Terah Lyons, James Manyika, Saurabh Mishra, and Juan Carlos Niebles, "The AI Index 2019 Annual Report," AI Index Steering Committee, Human-Centered AI Institute, Stanford University, Stanford, California, December 2019.

8. Saheli Roy Choudhury, "Chinese A.I. Company SenseTime Raises More than $1 Billion in Back-to-Back Funding Rounds," *CNBC.com.* Last modified, May 31, 2018. https://www.cnbc.com/2018/05/31/sensetime-raises-more-than-one-billion-dollars-in-mere-months.html.

9. https://openai.com/.

10. Press release. https://www2.deloitte.com/global/en/pages/about-deloitte/articles/deloitte-survey-only-eleven-percent-of-global-companies-report-repared-to-build-organization-future.html.

11. Dimple Agarwal, Josh Bersin, Gaurav Lahiri, "AI, Robotics, and Automation: Put Humans in the Loop," *Deloitte Insights, 2018 Global Human Capital Trends.* March 29, 2018. https://www2.deloitte.com/insights/us/en/focus/human-capital-trends/2018/ai-robotics-intelligent-machines.html.

12. Survey by Bitkom, German digital industry association, reported by Tobias Buck, "Germany to Spend €3bn on Boosting AI Capabilities," *Financial Times*, November 16, 2018. https://www.ft.com/content/fe1f9194-e8e3-11e8-a34c-663b3f553b35.

13. Aliya Ram, "Europe's AI Start-Ups Often Do Not Use AI, Study Says," *Financial Times*. March 4, 2019.

14. John Carreyrou, *Bad Blood: Secrets and Lies in a Silicon Valley Startup* (New York: Knopf, 2018).

15. The mission of Rasa, based in Germany, is to make scripted chatbots more conversational. https://rasa.com/.

16. Ilyse Liffreing, "Patch Is Using AI to Write 3,000 Articles a Week," *AdAge.com*, March 8, 2019. https://adage.com/article/digital/patch-ai-publish-3-000-articles-a-week/316914.

17. Katyanna Quach, "Experts Build AI Joke Machine that's about as Funny as an Adam Sandler Movie (That Bad)," *TheRegister.co.uk,* June

1, 2018. https://www.theregister.co.uk/2018/06/01/japanese_neural_network_jokes_comedy/.

18. Egor Zakharov, Aliaksandra Shysheya, Egor Burkov, Victor Lempitsky, "Few-Shot Adversarial Learning of Realistic Neural Talking Head Models," *ArXiv.org.* May 20, 2019. https://arxiv.org/pdf/1905.08233v1.pdf.

19. Also see Mariya Yao, Marlene Jia, Adelyn Zhou, *Applied Artificial Intelligence: A Handbook for Business Leaders* (TOPBOTS Inc., 2018).

20. See Frank Chen's video on a16z.com, "The Promise of AI," https://vimeo.com/215926017.

21. https://azure.microsoft.com/en-us/services/machine-learning-studio/.

22. https://www.microsoft.com/en-us/ai/ai-business-school.

23. Grace Dobush, "Microsoft Will Not Use Personal Data For Profit, Says Satya Nadella," *Fortune* (November 5, 2018).

24. https://ai.google/.

25. https://cloud.google.com/products/ai/.

26. https://www.coursera.org/.

27. https://aws.amazon.com/ai/.

28. https://www.research.ibm.com/artificial-intelligence/.

29. Q&A with Margaret Boden, *IBM—What's Next for AI?* https://www.ibm.com/watson/advantage-reports/future-of-artificial-intelligence/margaret-boden.html.

30. https://www.box.com/skills.

31. https://ai.facebook.com/tools/.

32. https://www.graphcore.ai/.

33. https://www.starkey.com/. Josh Dean, "The Ear Is the New Wrist," *Bloomberg Businessweek* (April 22, 2019), p. 58.

34. William M. Pride, O. C. Ferrell, *Marketing*, 18th ed. (Boston: Cengage Learning, 2016), p. 18.

35. Moody's senior vice president Neil Begley claims that Alphabet and Facebook "generate about two-thirds of global digital advertising revenue." Federica Cocco, "Digital Services Tax Is Credit Negative for Tech Giants—Moody's," *Financial Times*, November 5, 2018.

36. Matt Marshall, "For eBay, AI Drives Over $1 Billion in Sales per Quarter," *VentureBeat.com*, August 2, 2018. https://venturebeat.com/2018/08/02/for-ebay-ai-drives-over-1-billion-in-sales-per-quarter/.

37. https://www.adobe.com/sensei.html https://www.adobe.com/ analytics/adobe-analytics.html.

38. See Malcolm Frank, *What to Do When Machines Do Everything: How to Get Ahead in a World of AI, Algorithms, BOTs, and Big Data* (New York: Wiley, 2017).

39. https://www.conversica.com/ https://tact.ai/.

40. https://people.ai/.

41. https://www.salesforce.com/products/einstein/overview/.

42. https://www.qualtrics.com/.

43. Speech by Igor Jablokov, "Voice: The Key to Unlocking Business Value from Augmented Intelligence," AI Summit Conference, Jacob K. Javitz Convention Center, New York City, December 11–12, 2018. His new firm, Pryon, offers an augmented intelligence platform to boost workers' accuracy and productivity. https://www.pryon.com/.

44. No cited author, "The Five Ways AI Will Change US Healthcare in the Next Five Years," *Business Insider Intelligence,* June 1, 2018. https://www.businessinsider.com/five-ways-ai-change-us-healthcare-next-five-years-2018-6.

45. https://www.athenahealth.com/.

46. Jonathan Bush, "How AI Is Taking the Scut Work Out of Health Care," *Harvard Business Review*, March 5, 2018. https://store.hbr.org/product/how-ai-is-taking-the-scut-work-out-of-health-care/H046N5. Athenahealth was purchased in November 2018 by Veritas Capital and Elliott Management for $5.7 billion, at a 12 percent premium on the stock price.

47. https://verily.com/.

48. Jonathan Rabinovitz, "How Eric Horvitz's Artificial Intelligence Work Could Someday Save Your Life," *Stanford Magazine*, July 2018, pp. 59–63.

49. See AiCure to verify, using recorded evidence from a smartphone, that a med was taken. https://aicure.com/.

50. Qure.ai in Mumbai claims to be able to identify chest X-ray abnormalities at 90 percent accuracy and so increase the number of tuberculosis cases caught early, especially in poorer regions. It has received European CE certification from the European Medical Device Directive for this service. Based in Iowa, IDx raised $33 million to detect early eye diseases based on AI analysis of retinal images. https://www.eyediagnosis.net/.

51. https://corti.ai/.

52. https://www.orcam.com/en/.

53. Described in Polson and Scott, *AIQ*, p. 62. This app has been demonstrated to be as effective as the pill.

54. Brandon Sawalich, founder of Starkey Hearing Technologies, says, "The ear is the new wrist." See article by Josh Dean, *Bloomberg Businessweek*.

55. https://ceracare.co.uk/.

56. Anmar Frangoul, "Artificial Intelligence Is Helping to Transform the Way Elderly People Are Cared For," *CNBC.com*, May 3, 2018. https://www.cnbc.com/2018/05/03/ai-helping-to-transforming-elderly-health-care.html.

57. https://next.autonomous.com/augmented-finance-machine-intelligence.

58. Stephen Blyth, "Big Data and Machine Learning Won't Save Us from Another Financial Crisis," *Harvard Business Review*, September 18, 2018. https://hbr.org/2018/09/big-data-and-machine-learning-wont-save-us-from-another-financial-crisis?utm_campaign=Feed%3A+harvardbusiness+%28HBR.org%29&utm_medium=feed&utm_source=feedburner.

59. https://stripe.com/.

60. https://www.affirm.com/.

61. https://www.sitexpro.com/. See Kelsey Ramirez, "Black Knight Announces Acquisition to Incorporate AI into Its Solutions," *Housingwire.com*, June 4, 2018. https://www.housingwire.com/articles/43589-black-knight-announces-acquisition-to-incorporate-ai-into-its-solutions/.

62. https://www.mindbridge.ai/.

63. www.overbond.com. No cited author, "Artificial Intelligence May Change the Way Companies Issue Debt," *The Economist,* May 14, 2018. https://www.economist.com/graphic-detail/2018/05/14/artificial-intelligence-may-change-the-way-companies-issue-debt.

64. Eustance Huang, " 'AI Is Absolutely Critical for Us,' Ping An Technology CEO," *CNBC.com*, April 13, 2018. https://www.cnbc.com/2018/04/13/ai-is-absolutely-critical-for-us-ping-an-technology-ceo.html.

65. See Kittyhawk, a drone operations management company. Khari Johnson, "Kittyhawk Raises $3 Million to Expand Drone Use for Insurance Inspections," *VentureBeat.com*, October 3, 2018. https://

venturebeat.com/2018/10/03/kittyhawk-raises-3-million-to-expand-drone-use-for-insurance-inspections/.

66. https://www.amodo.eu/.

67. Marshall Allen, "Health Insurers Are Vacuuming Up Details about You—and It Could Raise Your Rates," *npr.org, Morning Edition*, July 17, 2018. https://www.npr.org/sections/health-shots/2018/07/17/629441555/health-insurers-are-vacuuming-up-details-about-you-and-it-could-raise-your-rates.

68. https://www.textrecruit.com/.

69. https://www.allyo.com/.

70. https://www.ultimatesoftware.com/UltiPro-Solution-Features-Xander-Perception.

71. https://www.pymetrics.com/employers/.

72. https://www.hirevue.com/.

73. Richard Feloni, "Consumer-Goods Giant Unilever Has Been Hiring Employees Using Brain Games and Artificial Intelligence—and It's a Huge Success," *Business Insider*, June 28, 2017. https://www.businessinsider.com/unilever-artificial-intelligence-hiring-process-2017-6. A case study of Unilever is available from the HireVue website.

74. https://www.darwinecosystem.com/.

75. Kyle Wiggers, "Darwin Ecosystem Uses AI to Help Police Departments Find Recruits Who Will Fit In," *VentureBeat.com*, June 11, 2018. https://venturebeat.com/2018/06/11/darwin-ecosystem-uses-ai-to-help-police-departments-find-recruits-wholl-fit-in/.

76. No cited author, "How artificial intelligence and machine learning are revolutionizing logistics, supply chain and transportation," *Forbes.com*, September 4, 2018. https://www.forbes.com/sites/insights-penske/2018/09/04/how-artificial-intelligence-and-machine-learning-are-revolutionizing-logistics-supply-chain-and-transportation/#2a17787258f5.

77. https://www.intelligrated.com/en https://www.transnorm.com/en/home.html.

78. https://www.tusimple.com/.

79. Check out Astro Aerospace's Elroy, Kitty Hawk's Cora, Workhorse's SureFly, Volocopter's 2X, Lilium's Jet, and EHang's 216.

80. Bernard Marr, "The Brilliant Ways UPS Uses Artificial Intelligence, Machine Learning and Big Data," *Forbes.com*, June 15, 2018. https://www.forbes.com/sites/bernardmarr/2018/06/15/the-brilliant-

ways-ups-uses-artificial-intelligence-machine-learning-and-big-data/
#277f6d35e6da.

81. https://www.mobileye.com/us/fleets/.

82. Shoshana Wodinsky, "Uber Wants to Patent a System that Knows When You're Drunk," *TheVerge.com*, June 8, 2018. https://www.theverge.com/2018/6/8/17441554/uber-drunk-passenger-ai.

83. http://sanalabs.com/.

84. Stephen Chen, "China's Schools Are Quietly Using AI to Mark Students' Essays . . . But Do the Robots Make the Grade?" *South China Morning Post*, May 27, 2018. https://www.scmp.com/news/china/society/article/2147833/chinas-schools-are-quietly-using-ai-mark-students-essays-do.

85. https://www.gaggle.net/.

86. https://www.securly.com/.

87. See Michelle Zimmerman, *Teaching AI: Exploring New Frontiers for Learning* (Arlington, VA: International Society for Technology in Education, 2018).

88. https://github.com/capitalone/AI_Dictionary_English_Spanish.

89. https://www.connecterra.io/.

90. http://www.taranis.ag/.

91. https://www.sigma-ai.com/.

92. https://www.eyesight-tech.com/.

93. https://go.affectiva.com/auto.

94. https://athena-security.com/. Hayley Leibson, "Female Founder Launches AI Security System that Helps Prevent School Shootings," *Forbes.com*, September 9, 2018. https://www.forbes.com/sites/hayleyleibson/2018/09/29/female-founder-launches-ai-security-system-that-helps-prevent-school-shootings/#e6c69841c6e5.

95. See Tim Bradshaw and Demetri Sevastopulo, "US Warns of Potential Data Leaks from Chinese-Made Drones," *Financial Times* (May 20, 2019). https://www.ft.com/content/b4193d5e-7b2b-11e9-81d2-f785092ab560.

96. https://flyzipline.com/. See Martin Giles, "Zipline Launches the World's Fastest Commercial Delivery Drone," *MIT Technology Review* (April 30, 2018). https://www.technologyreview.com/s/610735/zipline-launches-the-worlds-fastest-commercial-delivery-drone/.

97. https://www.shield.ai/.

98. https://www.nasa.gov/subject/9566/unmanned-aircraft/. Also see Scott Sonner, "NASA First-of-Kind Tests Looks to Manage Drones in Cities," *Associated Press* (May 24, 2019).

99. https://www.darktrace.com/en/.

100. https://clarifai.com/.

101. Quote from US Supreme Court Justice Potter Stewart in *Jacobellis vs. Ohio* (1964).

102. Speech by Brigadier General R. Patrick Huston, Commander, Judge Advocate General Legal Center, given at Stanford Law School, April 2019.

103. See Jack Poulson's August 20, 2018, resignation letter, https://www.documentcloud.org/documents/4905801-Jack-Poulson-Google-resignation-letter-20-Aug-2018.html, and his letter to the US Senate committee on commerce, science, and transportation, dated September 24, 2018, https://www.documentcloud.org/documents/4941446-Jack-Poulson-Letter-to-Senate-Commerce-Committee.html.

104. https://www.radiantsolutions.com/ Press release, "Maxar's radiant solutions selected by DARPA to develop next-generation optical system for agile earth observation satellites," *investor.maxar.com,* November 8, 2018. http://investor.maxar.com/investor-news/press-release-details/2018/Maxars-Radiant-Solutions-Selected-by-DARPA-to-Develop-Next-Generation-Optical-System-for-Agile-Earth-Observation-Satellites/default.aspx.

105. https://www.uptake.com/.

106. James Vincent, "The US Army Is Using Machine Learning to Predict When Combat Vehicles Need Repair," *TheVerge.com,* June 26, 2018. https://www.theverge.com/2018/6/26/17506170/us-army-machine-learning-ai-predict-vehicle-failure-uptake-technologies.

4. AI SUCCESS IN YOUR ORGANIZATION

1. Ritu Jyoti, "IDC Survey: Artificial Intelligence Global Adoption Trends & Strategies," International Data Corporation, online presentation, accessed July 23, 2019. https://www.idc.com/getdoc.jsp?containerId=US45120919. Summary found in Gil Press, "This Week in AI Stats: Up to 50% Failure Rate in 25% of Enterprises Deploying AI," *Forbes,* July 19, 2019. https://www.forbes.com/sites/gilpress/2019/07/19/

this-week-in-ai-stats-up-to-50-failure-rate-in-25-of-enterprises-deploying-ai/#589ffaf572ce.

2. Quoted in Khari Johnson, "Cloudera's Hilary Mason on How Businesses Can Avoid Ruining Their Own AI Projects," *VentureBeat*, July 12, 2019. https://venturebeat.com/2019/07/12/clouderas-hilary-mason-on-how-businesses-can-avoid-ruining-their-own-ai-projects/.

3. Giancarlo Valdes, "To Be Successful with AI, You Have to Start Small," *VentureBeat*, July 12, 2019. https://venturebeat.com/2019/07/12/to-be-successful-with-ai-you-have-to-start-small/.

4. Thomas M. Siebel, *Digital Transformation: Survive and Thrive in an Era of Mass Extinction* (New York: Rosetta Books, 2019), p. 177.

5. For advice on how to address AI in the corporate boardroom, see Anastassia Lauterbach and Andrea Bonime-Blanc, *The Artificial Intelligence Imperative: A Practical Roadmap for Business* (Santa Barbara, CA: Praeger, ABC-CLIO, 2018), pp. 233–40

6. See https://docs.rundexter.com/ for full information about how to code a bot and add many features.

7. For an interview with Telefónica's CDO Chema Alonso about Aura, see https://docs.microsoft.com/en-us/learn/modules/ai-strategy-to-create-business-value/4-transform-applications-executive-qa. Also see https://aura.telefonica.com.

5. AI GOVERNANCE
AND DATA CONTROLS

1. http://longnow.org/.

2. Kevin Kelly, "The Myth of a Superhuman AI," *Wired*, Backchannel, April 25, 2017.

3. Jared Council, "Data Challenges Are Halting AI Projects, IBM Executive Says," *Wall Street Journal*, May 28, 2019.

4. "Why We Need to Understand Science," *The Skeptical Inquirer*, Vol. 14, Issue 3 (Spring 1990).

BIBLIOGRAPHY

BOOKS AND ARTICLES

Agarwal, Dimple, Josh Bersin, and Gaurav Lahiri. "AI, Robotics, and Automation: Put Humans in the Loop." *Deloitte Insights, 2018 Global Human Capital Trends.* March 29, 2018. https://www2.deloitte.com/insights/us/en/focus/human-capital-trends/2018/ai-robotics-intelligent-machines.html.

Agrawal, Ajay, Joshua Gans, and Avi Goldfarb. *Prediction Machines: The Simple Economics of Artificial Intelligence.* Boston: Harvard Business Review Press, 2018.

Agusti, Solanas, et al. *Advances in Artificial Intelligence for Privacy Protection and Security.* Singapore; River Edge, NJ: World Scientific, 2009. eBook.

Allen, Marshall. "Health Insurers Are Vacuuming Up Details about You—and It Could Raise Your Rates." *Npr.org, Morning Edition.* July 17, 2018. https://www.npr.org/sections/health-shots/2018/07/17/629441555/health-insurers-are-vacuuming-up-details-about-you-and-it-could-raise-your-rates.

Allenby, Braden R., and Daniel R. Sarewitz. *The Techno-Human Condition.* Cambridge, MA: MIT Press, 2011. eBook.

Alonso, Chema. Interview about Telefónica's Aura. https://docs.microsoft.com/en-us/learn/modules/ai-strategy-to-create-business-value/4-transform-applications-executive-qa.

Alsinet, Teresa, J. Puyol-Gruart, and C. Torras. *Artificial Intelligence Research and Development.* Amsterdam: IOS Press, 2008. eBook.

Anderson, Michael, and Susan Leigh Anderson. *Machine Ethics.* Leiden, Netherlands: Cambridge University Press, 2011. eBook.

Aoun, Joseph. *Robot-Proof: Higher Education in the Age of Artificial Intelligence.* Cambridge, MA: MIT Press, 2017.

Awret, Uziel. *The Singularity: Could Artificial Intelligence Really Out-Think Us (and Would We Want It To)?* Luton, UK: Imprint Academic, 2016. eBook.

Baker, Stephen. *Final Jeopardy: Man vs. Machine and the Quest to Know Everything.* Boston: Houghton Mifflin Harcourt, 2011.

Beck, Megan, Thomas H. Davenport, and Barry Libert. "The AI Roles Some Companies Forget to Fill." *Harvard Business Review Digital Articles,* March 2–5, 2019.

Berlatsky, Noah. *Artificial Intelligence.* Detroit, MI: Greenhaven Press, 2011.

Bharath, A. A., and Maria Petrou. *Next-Generation Artificial Vision Systems: Reverse Engineering the Human Visual System*. Boston: Artech House, 2008. eBook.

Blackford, Russell, and Damien Broderick. *Intelligence Unbound: The Future of Uploaded and Machine Minds*. Chichester, West Sussex, UK: John Wiley & Sons, Inc., 2014. eBook.

Blyth, Stephen. "Big Data and Machine Learning Won't Save Us from Another Financial Crisis." *Harvard Business Review*. September 18, 2018. https://hbr.org/2018/09/big-data-and-machine-learning-wont-save-us-from-another-financial-crisis?utm_campaign=Feed%3A+harvardbusiness+%28HBR.org%29&utm_medium=feed&utm_source=feedburner.

Boden, Margaret A. *AI: Its Nature and Future*. Oxford, UK: Oxford University Press, 2016. eBook.

Bostrom, Nick. *Superintelligence: Paths, Dangers, Strategies*. Oxford, UK: Oxford University Press, 2014. eBook.

Bradshaw, Tim, and Demetri Sevastopulo. "US Warns of Potential Data Leaks from Chinese-Made Drones." *Financial Times*. May 20, 2019.

Brey, Philip, Adam Briggle, and Katinka Waelbers. *Current Issues in Computing and Philosophy*. Amsterdam: Ios Press, 2008. eBook.

Brock, Brian. *Christian Ethics in a Technological Age*. Grand Rapids, MI; Cambridge, UK: William B. Eerdmans Publishing Company, 2010.

Buck, Tobias. "Germany to Spend €3bn on Boosting AI Capabilities." *Financial Times*. November 16, 2018.

Bush, Jonathan. "How AI Is Taking the Scut Work Out of Health Care." *Harvard Business Review*. March 5, 2018.

Carreyrou, John. *Bad Blood: Secrets and Lies in a Silicon Valley Startup*. New York: Knopf, 2018.

Carter, Matt. *Minds and Computers: An Introduction to the Philosophy of Artificial Intelligence*. Edinburgh: Edinburgh University Press, 2007. eBook.

Chen, Stephen. "China's Schools Are Quietly Using AI to Mark Students' Essays . . . But Do the Robots Make the Grade?" *South China Morning Post*. May 27, 2018. https://www.scmp.com/news/china/society/article/2147833/chinas-schools-are-quietly-using-ai-mark-students-essays-do.

Cheng, Evelyn. "A.I. Could Spur Global Growth as Much as the Steam Engine Did, Study Shows." *CNBC.com*. Last modified September 5, 2018. https://www.cnbc.com/2018/09/05/artificial-intelligence-ai-could-spur-global-growth-study-shows.html.

Chong, Nak-Young. *Networking Humans, Robots and Environments*. Oak Park, IL: Bentham Science Publishers, 2013. eBook.

Choudhury, Saheli Roy. "Chinese A.I. Company SenseTime Raises More than $1 Billion in Back-to-Back Funding Rounds." *CNBC.com*. Last modified May 31, 2018. https://www.cnbc.com/2018/05/31/sensetime-raises-more-than-one-billion-dollars-in-mere-months.html.

Christian, Brian. *The Most Human Human: What Talking with Computers Teaches Us about What It Means to Be Alive*. Cambridge, MA; London, England: MIT Press, 2012.

Clark, Andy. *Natural-Born Cyborgs: Minds, Technologies, and the Future of Human Intelligence*. Oxford; New York: Oxford University Press, 2003. eBook.

Cocco, Federica. "Digital Services Tax Is Credit Negative for Tech Giants— Moody's." *Financial Times*. November 5, 2018.

Cookson, Clive. "Huge Surge in AI Patent Applications in Past 5 Years." *Financial Times*. January 31, 2019.

Council, Jared. "Data Challenges Are Halting AI Projects, IBM Executive Says." *Wall Street Journal*. May 28, 2019.

Cunningham, Anne C. *Artificial Intelligence and the Technological Singularity*. New York: Greenhaven Publishing, 2017.

Daugherty, Paul R., and H. James Wilson. *Human + Machine: Reimagining Work in the Age of AI*. Boston: Harvard Business Review Press, 2018. eBook.

Davenport, Thomas H. *The AI Advantage: How to Put the Artificial Intelligence Revolution to Work*. Cambridge, MA: MIT Press, 2018.

Davim, J. Paulo. *Artificial Intelligence in Manufacturing Research*. New York: Nova Science Publishers, 2010. eBook.

Davis, Kim, ed. *The Promises and Perils of Modern AI*. Fort Atkinson, WI: DMN, 2018. eBook.

Dawson, Michael, Brian Dupuis, and Michael Wilson. *From Bricks to Brains: The Embodied Cognitive Science of Lego Robots*. Edmonton, Alberta, Canada: Athabasca University Press, 2014. eBook.

Dean, Josh. "The Ear Is the New Wrist." *Bloomberg Businessweek*. April 22, 2019.

Dedezade, Esat. "Leaders Look to Embrace AI, and High-Growth Companies Are Seeing the Benefits." *Microsoft News Centre Europe*, March 5, 2019. https://news. microsoft.com/europe/features/leaders-look-to-embrace-ai-and-high-growth-companies-are-seeing-the-benefits/.

De Gyurky, Szabolcs Michael, and Mark A. Tarbell. *The Autonomous System: A Foundational Synthesis of the Sciences of the Mind*. Hoboken, NJ: Wiley, 2014. eBook.

DeLancey, Craig. *Passionate Engines: What Emotions Reveal about the Mind and Artificial Intelligence*. Cary, NC: Oxford University Press, 2004. eBook.

Dickie, Jim. "Small Businesses, Take Note: AI Is Ready for Prime Time: It's Not Just for Big Enterprises Anymore. Even Mom-and-Pop Shops Can Use AI to Optimize Sales." *CRM Magazine* 22 (10) (December 2018). https://www.destinationcrm. com/Articles/ReadArticle.aspx?ArticleID=128722.

Dobush, Grace. "Microsoft Will Not Use Personal Data for Profit, Says Satya Nadella." *Fortune*. November 5, 2018.

Dodigovic, Marina. *Artificial Intelligence in Second Language Learning: Raising Error Awareness*. Clevedon, England: Multilingual Matters, 2005. eBook.

Doumpos, Michael, and Evangelos Grigoroudis. *Multicriteria Decision Aid and Artificial Intelligence: Links, Theory and Applications*. Hoboken, NJ: Wiley-Blackwell, 2013.

Duro, Richard, Yuriy Kondratenko, and Richard J. Duro. *Advances in Intelligent Robotics and Collaborative Automation.* Aalborg, Denmark: River Publishers, 2015. eBook.

Epstein, Robert S., Gary Roberts, PhD, and Grace Beber. *Parsing the Turing Test: Philosophical and Methodological Issues in the Quest for the Thinking Computer*. Dordrecht; London: Springer, 2009. eBook.

Feloni, Richard. "Consumer-Goods Giant Unilever Has Been Hiring Employees Using Brain Games and Artificial Intelligence—and It's a Huge Success." *Business Insider*. June 28, 2017. https://www.businessinsider.com/unilever-artificial-intelligence-hiring-process-2017-6.

Finlay, Steven. *Artificial Intelligence and Machine Learning for Business: A No-Nonsense Guide to Data-Driven Technologies*, 2nd ed. Relativistic, 2017.

Finn, Ed. *What Algorithms Want: Imagination in the Age of Computing*. Cambridge, MA: MIT Press, 2017.

Floreano, Dario, and Claudio Mattiussi. *Bio-Inspired Artificial Intelligence: Theories, Methods, and Technologies*. Cambridge, MA: MIT Press, 2008. eBook.

Flores, John A. *Focus on Artificial Neural Networks*. New York: Nova Science Publishers, 2011. eBook.

Frangoul, Anmar. "Artificial Intelligence Is Helping to Transform the Way Elderly People Are Cared For." *CNBC.com*. May 3, 2018. https://www.cnbc.com/2018/05/03/ai-helping-to-transforming-elderly-health-care.html.

Frank, Malcolm. *What to Do When Machines Do Everything: How to Get Ahead in a World of AI, Algorithms, BOTs, and Big Data*. New York: Wiley, 2017.

Frey, Carl Benedikt. *The Technology Trap: Capital, Labor, and Power in the Age of Automation*. Princeton, NJ: Princeton University Press, 2019.

Gavri'el Haleyi. *When Robots Kill: Artificial Intelligence under Criminal Law*. Boston: Northeastern University Press, 2013. eBook.

Geng Cui, and Man Leung Wong. "Implementing Neural Networks for Decision Support in Direct Marketing." *International Journal of Market Research* 46 (2004): 235–54. https://doi.org/10.1177/147078530404600204.

Geraci, Robert M. *Apocalyptic AI: Visions of Heaven in Robotics, Artificial Intelligence, and Virtual Reality*. Oxford; New York: Oxford University Press, 2010. eBook.

Goertzel, B., and P. Wang. *Advances in Artificial General Intelligence: Concepts, Architectures and Algorithms*. Amsterdam: Ios Press, 2007. eBook.

Ghosh, Bhaskar, Paul R. Daugherty, H. James Wilson, and Adam Burden. "Taking a Systems Approach to Adopting AI." *Harvard Business Review Digital Articles*, May 2–6, 2019.

Gift, Noah. *Pragmatic AI: An Introduction to Cloud-Based Machine Learning*. Boston: Addison Wesley, 2019.

Giles, Martin. "Zipline Launches the World's Fastest Commercial Delivery Drone." *MIT Technology Review*. April 30, 2018. https://www.technologyreview.com/s/610735/zipline-launches-the-worlds-fastest-commercial-delivery-drone/.

González, Evelio J. *Artificial Intelligence Resources in Control and Automation Engineering*. Sharjah, United Arab Emirates: Bentham Science Publishers, 2012. eBook.

Gordon, Brent M. *Artificial Intelligence: Approaches, Tools, and Applications*. New York: Nova Science Publishers, 2011. eBook.

Grace, David, and Honggang Zhang. *Cognitive Communications: Distributed Artificial Intelligence (DAI), Regulatory Policy and Economics, Implementation*. Hoboken, NJ: Wiley, 2012. eBook.

Haenlein, Michael, and Andreas Kaplan. "A Brief History of Artificial Intelligence: On the Past, Present, and Future of Artificial Intelligence." *California Management Review*, 10 (2018).

Hall, J. Storrs. *Beyond AI: Creating the Conscience of the Machine*. Amherst, NY: Prometheus Books, 2007.

Hawkins, William M. *Automating Manufacturing Operations: The Penultimate Approach*. New York: Momentum Press, 2013. eBook.

Helen, Morten, and Aleksander Igor. *Aristotle's Laptop: The Discovery of Our Informational Mind*. Singapore; River Edge, NJ: World Scientific, 2012. eBook.

Henschke, Adam. *Ethics in an Age of Surveillance: Personal Information and Virtual Identities*. Cambridge, UK: Cambridge University Press, 2017.

Herper, Matthew. "MD Anderson Benches IBM Watson in Setback for Artificial Intelligence in Medicine." *Forbes.com*. February 19, 2017. https://www.forbes.com/sites/matthewherper/2017/02/19/md-anderson-benches-ibm-watson-in-setback-for-artificial-intelligence-in-medicine/#3175068f3774.

Huang, Eustance. "'AI Is Absolutely Critical for Us,' Ping An Technology CEO." *CNBC.com*. April 13, 2018. https://www.cnbc.com/2018/04/13/ai-is-absolutely-critical-for-us-ping-an-technology-ceo.html.

Hurwitz, Judith, Marcia Kaufman, and Adrian Bowles. *Cognitive Computing and Big Data Analytics*. Hoboken, NJ: Wiley, 2015. eBook.

Husbands, Phil, Owen Holland, and Michael Wheeler. *The Mechanical Mind in History*. Cambridge, MA; London: MIT, 2008. eBook.

Huston, R. Patrick, Brigadier General, Commander. Speech given at Judge Advocate General Legal Center, Stanford Law School, April 2019.

Jablokov, Igor. "Voice: The Key to Unlocking Business Value from Augmented Intelligence." Conference presentation at AI Summit Conference, Jacob K. Javitz Convention Center, New York City. December 11–12, 2018.

Johnson, Khari. "Kittyhawk Raises $3 Million to Expand Drone Use for Insurance Inspections." *VentureBeat.com*. October 3, 2018. https://venturebeat.com/2018/10/03/kittyhawk-raises-3-million-to-expand-drone-use-for-insurance-inspections/.

———. "Cloudera's Hilary Mason on How Businesses Can Avoid Ruining Their Own AI Projects." *VentureBeat.com*. July 12, 2019.

Johnston, Casey. "Netflix Never Used Its $1 Million Algorithm Due to Engineering Costs." *Ars Technica*. Last modified April 16, 2012. https://www.wired.com/2012/04/netflix-prize-costs/.

Johnston, John. *The Allure of Machinic Life: Cybernetics, Artificial Life, and the New AI*. Cambridge, MA: MIT Press, 2008. eBook.

Jyoti, Ritu. "IDC Survey: Artificial Intelligence Global Adoption Trends & Strategies." International Data Corporation, online presentation, accessed July 23, 2019. https://www.idc.com/getdoc.jsp?containerId=US45120919.

Kelly, Kevin. "The Myth of a Superhuman AI." *Wired*, Backchannel. April 25, 2017.

Kelly III, John E., and Steve Hamm. *Smart Machines: IBM's Watson and the Era of Cognitive Computing*. New York: Columbia University Press, 2013. eBook.

Kitamura, Tadashi. *What Should Be Computed to Understand and Model Brain function? From Robotics, Soft Computing, Biology and Neuroscience to Cognitive Philosophy*. Singapore; River Edge, NJ: World Scientific, 2001. eBook.

Kokina, Julia, and Thomas H. Davenport. "The Emergence of Artificial Intelligence: How Automation Is Changing Auditing." *Journal of Emerging Technologies in Accounting* 14-1 (2017): 115–22. https://doi.org/10.2308/jeta-51730.

Konar, Amit, and Aruna Chakraborty. *Emotion Recognition: A Pattern Analysis Approach*. Hoboken, NJ: Wiley, 2014. eBook.

Kopec, Danny, Christopher Pileggi, David M. Ungar, and Shweta Shetty. *Artificial Intelligence and Problem Solving*. Dulles, VA: Mercury Learning and Information, 2017.

Kulkarni , Sanjeev, and Gilbert Harman. *An Elementary Introduction to Statistical Learning Theory*. Hoboken, NJ: Wiley, 2011. eBook.

Kyaw, Aung Sithu, and Thet Naing Swe. *Unity 4.x Game AI Programming*. Birmingham, UK: Packt Publishing, 2013. eBook.

Laird, John. *The Soar Cognitive Architecture*. Cambridge, MA; London, England: MIT Press, 2012. eBook.

Lajoie, S. P., and M. Vivet. *Artificial Intelligence in Education*. Amsterdam: IOS Press, 2002. eBook.

Lam, H. K., San Ling, and Hung T. Nguyen. *Computational Intelligence and Its Applications: Evolutionary Computation, Fuzzy Logic, Neural Network and Support Vector Machine Techniques*. London, UK: Imperial College Press; Singapore: Dist. by World Scientific, 2012. eBook.

Lauterbach, Anastassia, and Andrea Bonime-Blanc. *The Artificial Intelligence Imperative: A Practical Roadmap for Business*. Santa Barbara, CA: Praeger, an imprint of ABC-CLIO, LLC, 2018.

Lee, Kai-Fu. *AI Superpowers: China, Silicon Valley, and the New World Order*. New York: Houghton Mifflin Harcourt, 2018.

Leibson, Hayley. "Female Founder Launches AI Security System that Helps Prevent School Shootings." *Forbes.com*. September 9, 2018. https://www.forbes.com/sites/

hayleyleibson/2018/09/29/female-founder-launches-ai-security-system-that-helps-prevent-school-shootings/#e6c69841c6e5.

Liffreing, Ilyse. "Patch Is Using AI to Write 3,000 Articles a Week." *AdAge.com*, March 8, 2019. https://adage.com/article/digital/patch-ai-publish-3-000-articles-a-week/316914.

Lin, Lin, and Mitsuo Gen. "Hybrid Evolutionary Optimisation with Learning for Production Scheduling: State-of-the-Art Survey on Algorithms and Applications." *International Journal of Production Research* 56 (2018): 193–223. https://doi.org/10.1080/00207543.2018.1437288.

Lodder, A. R., and L. Mommers. *Legal Knowledge and Information Systems*. Amsterdam: IOS Press, 2007. eBook.

Lorrentz, Pierre. *Artificial Neural Systems: Principles and Practice*. Oak Park, IL: Bentham Science Publishers, 2015. eBook.

Maglogiannis, I., K. Karpouzis, and M. Wallace. *Emerging Artificial Intelligence Applications in Computer Engineering: Real-World AI Systems with Applications in eHealth, HCI, Information Retrieval and Pervasive Technologies*. Amsterdam: IOS Press, 2007. eBook.

Magnuson, Stew. "DARPA Spending $2 Billion to Advance AI Technologies." *NationalDefenseMagazine.org*. September 7, 2018. http://www.nationaldefensemagazine.org/articles/2018/9/7/darpa-spending-$2-billion-to-advance-ai-technologies.

Mahfouf, Mahdi. *Intelligent Systems Modeling and Decision Support in Bioengineering*. Boston: Artech House, 2006. eBook.

Marr, Bernard. "The Brilliant Ways UPS Uses Artificial Intelligence, Machine Learning and Big Data." *Forbes.com*. June 15, 2018. https://www.forbes.com/sites/bernardmarr/2018/06/15/the-brilliant-ways-ups-uses-artificial-intelligence-machine-learning-and-big-data/#277f6d35e6da.

Marshall, Matt. "For eBay, AI Drives Over $1 Billion in Sales per Quarter." *VentureBeat.com*. August 2, 2018. https://venturebeat.com/2018/08/02/for-ebay-ai-drives-over-1-billion-in-sales-per-quarter/.

Maulik, Ujjwal, Sanghamitra Bandyopadhyay, and Jason T. L. Wang. *Computational Intelligence and Pattern Analysis in Biology Informatics*. Hoboken, NJ: Wiley, 2010. eBook.

McCarthy, J., M. L. Minsky, N. Rochester, C. E. Shannon. "A Proposal for the Dartmouth Summer Research Project on Artificial Intelligence." August 31, 1955. Last modified April 3, 1996. http://www-formal.stanford.edu/jmc/history/dartmouth/dartmouth.html.

Meyer, Cheryl. "How We Successfully Implemented AI in Audit." *Journal of Accountancy* 227 (2019): 1–3.

Murgia, Madhumita. "How to Stop Computers Being Biased: The Bid to Prevent Algorithms Producing Racist, Sexist or Class-Conscious Decisions." *Financial Times*. February 12, 2019.

Ng, G. W. *Brain-Mind Machinery: Brain-Inspired Computing and Mind Opening*. Singapore; River Edge, NJ: World Scientific, 2009. eBook.

Noyer, Jean-Max. *Transformation of Collective Intelligences: Perspective of Transhumanism*. London: Wiley, 2016. eBook.

OECD. "Private Equity Investment in Artificial Intelligence." *OECD Going Digital Policy Note*. OECD, Paris. December 2018. http://www.oecd.org/going-digital/ai/private-equity-investment-in-artificial-intelligence.pdf.

O'Neil, Cathy. *Weapons of Math Destruction: How Big Data Increases Inequality and Threatens Democracy*. New York: Broadway Books, 2016.

Pan, Yi, Jianxin Wang, and Min Li. *Algorithmic and Artificial Intelligence Methods for Protein Bioinformatics*. Hoboken, NJ: Wiley, 2014. eBook.

Parisi, Domenico. *Future Robots: Towards a Robotic Science of Human Beings.* Amsterdam; Philadelphia: John Benjamins Publishing Company, 2014. eBook.

Pereira, Francisco Câmara. *Creativity and Artificial Intelligence: A Conceptual Blending Approach.* Berlin, Germany: Walter de Gruyter, 2008. eBook.

Perrault, Raymond, Yoav Shoham, Erik Brynjolfsson, Jack Clark, John Etchemendy, Barbara Grosz, Terah Lyons, James Manyika, Saurabh Mishra, and Juan Carlos Niebles. *The AI Index 2019 Annual Report.* Stanford, CA: AI Index Steering Committee, Human-Centered AI Institute, Stanford University, December 2019.

Pitrat, J. *Artificial Beings: The Conscience of a Conscious Machine.* London: ISTE; Hoboken, NJ: Wiley, 2009. eBook.

Polson, Nicholas G., and James Scott. *AIQ: How People and Machines Are Smarter Together.* New York: St. Martin's Press, 2018.

Press, Gil. "This Week in AI Stats: Up to 50% Failure Rate in 25% of Enterprises Deploying AI." *Forbes.com.* July 19, 2019. https://www.forbes.com/sites/gilpress/2019/07/19/this-week-in-ai-stats-up-to-50-failure-rate-in-25-of-enterprises-deploying-ai/#589ffaf572ce.

Pride, William M., and O. C. Ferrell. *Marketing,* 18th ed. Boston: Cengage Learning, 2016.

Quach, Katyanna. "Experts Build AI Joke Machine That's About as Funny as an Adam Sandler Movie (That Bad)." *TheRegister.co.uk.* June 1, 2018. https://www.theregister.co.uk/2018/06/01/japanese_neural_network_jokes_comedy/.

Quan-Haase, Anabel. *Technology & Society: Social Networks, Power, and Inequality,* 2nd ed. Oxford, UK: Oxford University Press, 2016.

Rabinovitz, Jonathan. "How Eric Horvitz's Artificial Intelligence Work Could Someday Save Your Life." *Stanford Magazine.* July 2018. pp. 59–63.

Ram, Aliya. "Europe's AI Start-Ups Often Do Not Use AI, Study Says." *Financial Times.* March 4, 2019.

Ramirez, Kelsey. "Black Knight Announces Acquisition to Incorporate AI into Its Solutions." *Housingwire.com.* June 4, 2018.

Ransbotham, Sam, Philipp Gerbert, Martin Reeves, David Kiron, and Michael Spira. "Artificial Intelligence in Business Gets Real." *MIT Sloan Management Review.* September 17, 2018. https://sloanreview.mit.edu/projects/artificial-intelligence-in-business-gets-real/.

Rasskin-Gutman, Diego. *Chess Metaphors: Artificial Intelligence and the Human Mind.* Cambridge, MA: MIT Press, 2009. eBook.

Riaño, D., E. Onaindia, and M. Cazorla. *Artificial Intelligence Research and Development.* Amsterdam: IOS Press, 2012. eBook.

Riesen, Kaspar, and Horst Bunke. *Graph Classification and Clustering Based on Vector Space Embedding.* Singapore; River Edge, NJ: World Scientific, 2010. eBook.

Rondeau, Thomas W., and Charles W. Bostian. *Artificial Intelligence in Wireless Communications.* Norwood, MA: Artech House, 2009. eBook.

Russell, Stuart. *Human Compatible: Artificial Intelligence and the Problem of Control.* New York: Viking (Penguin), 2019.

Sarvady, Glen. "Chatbots, Robo Advisers, & AI: Technologies Presage an Enhanced Member Experience, Improved Sales, and Lower Costs." *Credit Union Magazine* 83 (2017): 18–22.

Sebastian, D. J. *The Selling Revolution: Prospering in the New World of Artificial Intelligence.* Samuelson Publishing, 2019.

Shanahan, Murray. *The Technological Singularity.* Cambridge, MA: MIT Press, 2015. eBook.

Shi Zhongzhi. *Advanced Artificial Intelligence.* Singapore; River Edge, NJ: World Scientific, 2011. eBook.

Siebel, Thomas M. *Digital Transformation: Survive and Thrive in an Era of Mass Extinction*. New York: Rosetta Books, 2019.

Solove, Daniel J. *Understanding Privacy*. Cambridge, MA: Harvard University Press, 2008.

Sonner, Scott. "NASA First-of-Kind Tests Look to Manage Drones in Cities." *Associated Press*. May 24, 2019.

Sra, Suvrit, Sebastian Nowozin, and Stephen J. Wright. *Optimization for Machine Learning*. Cambridge, MA: MIT Press, 2012. eBook.

Stathopoulou, Ioanna-Ourania, and George A. Tsihrintzis. *Visual Affect Recognition*. Washington, DC: IOS Press, 2010. eBook.

Sugiyama, Masashi, and Motoaki Kawanabe. *Machine Learning in Non-Stationary Environments: Introduction to Covariate Shift Adaptation*. Cambridge, MA: MIT Press, 2012. eBook.

Swirski, Peter. *From Literature to Biterature: Lem, Turing, Darwin, and Explorations in Computer Literature, Philosophy of Mind, and Cultural Evolution*. Montreal: McGill–Queen's University Press, 2013. eBook.

Tegmark, Max. *Life 3.0: Being Human in the Age of Artificial Intelligence*. New York: Alfred A. Knopf, 2017.

Topol, Eric. *Deep Medicine: How Artificial Intelligence Can Make Healthcare Human Again*. New York: Basic Books, 2019.

Tōugu, Enn. *Algorithms and Architectures of Artificial Intelligence*. Amsterdam; Oxford: IOS Press, 2007. eBook.

Uchyigit, Gulden, and Matthew Y. Ma. *Personalization Techniques and Recommender Systems*. Singapore; River Edge, NJ: World Scientific, 2008. eBook.

Valdes, Giancarlo. "To Be Successful with AI, You Have to Start Small." *VentureBeat.com*. July 12, 2019.

Vallor, Shannon. *Technology and the Virtues: A Philosophical Guide to a Future Worth Wanting*. Oxford: Oxford University Press, 2016.

Vernon, David. *Artificial Cognitive Systems: A Primer*. Cambridge, MA: MIT Press, 2014. eBook.

Vincent, James. "The US Army Is Using Machine Learning to Predict When Combat Vehicles Need Repair." *TheVerge.com*. June 26, 2018. https://www.theverge.com/2018/6/26/17506170/us-army-machine-learning-ai-predict-vehicle-failure-uptake-technologies.

Walker, Joshua H. *On Legal AI*. Washington, DC: Full Court Press, Fastcase Inc., 2019.

Wan, Shibiao, and M. W. Mak. *Machine Learning for Protein Subcellular Localization Prediction*. Berlin, Germany; Boston, Massachusetts: De Gruyter, 2015. eBook.

Wang, Pei. *Non-Axiomatic Logic: A Model of Intelligent Reasoning*. Singapore; River Edge, NJ: World Scientific, 2013. eBook.

Warwick, K. *Artificial Intelligence: The Basics*. New York: Routledge, 2012. eBook.

Weiss, Gerhard. *Multiagent Systems*. Cambridge, MA; London, England: MIT Press, 2013. eBook.

West, Darrell M. *The Future of Work: Robots, AI, and Automation*. Washington, DC: Brookings Institution Press, 2018. eBook.

Wichert, Andreas. *Principles of Quantum Artificial Intelligence*. Singapore; River Edge, NJ: World Scientific, 2013. eBook.

Wiggers, Kyle. "Darwin Ecosystem Uses AI to Help Police Departments Find Recruits Who Will Fit In." *VentureBeat.com*. June 11, 2018. https://venturebeat.com/2018/06/11/darwin-ecosystem-uses-ai-to-help-police-departments-find-recruits-wholl-fit-in/.

Wilks, Yorick. *Close Engagements with Artificial Companions: Key Social, Psychological, Ethical and Design Issues*. Amsterdam; Philadelphia, PA: John Benjamins Publishing, 2010. eBook.

Wilson, Elizabeth A. *Affect and Artificial Intelligence*. Seattle: University of Washington Press, 2010. eBook.

Wodinsky, Shoshana. "Uber Wants to Patent a System that Knows When You're Drunk." *TheVerge.com.* June 8, 2018. https://www.theverge.com/2018/6/8/17441554/uber-drunk-passenger-ai.

Yampolskiy, Roman V. *Artificial Superintelligence: A Futuristic Approach*. Boca Raton, FL: CRC Press / Taylor & Francis Group, 2016.

———. *Artificial Intelligence Safety and Security*. Boca Raton, FL: CRC Press / Taylor & Francis Group, 2018.

Yao, Mariya, Marlene Jia, Adelyn Zhou, and Natalia Zhang. *Applied Artificial Intelligence: A Handbook for Business Leaders*. Middletown, DE: TOPBOTS, 2018.

Zakharov, Egor, Aliaksandra Shysheya, Egor Burkov, and Victor Lempitsky. "Few-Shot Adversarial Learning of Realistic Neural Talking Head Models." *ArXiv.org.* May 20, 2019. https://arxiv.org/pdf/1905.08233v1.pdf.

Zimmerman, Michelle Renée. "Why We Need to Understand Science." *The Skeptical Inquirer*. Vol. 14, Issue 3 (Spring 1990).

———. *Teaching AI: Exploring New Frontiers for Learning*. Portland, OR: International Society for Technology in Education, 2018.

WEBSITES

Adobe—Analytics. https://www.adobe.com/analytics/adobe-analytics.html.

Adobe—Sensei. https://www.adobe.com/sensei.html.

Affectiva Automotive AI. https://go.affectiva.com/auto.

Affirm. https://www.affirm.com/.

AiCure. https://aicure.com/.

Allyo. https://www.allyo.com/.

Amazon—Machine Learning on AWS. https://aws.amazon.com/ai/.

Amodo. https://www.amodo.eu/.

Andreessen Horowitz: Software is eating the world. https://a16z.com/.

Athena. https://athena-security.com/.

AthenaHealth. https://www.athenahealth.com/.

Autonomous Next. https://next.autonomous.com/augmented-finance-machine-intelligence.

Box—Skills. https://www.box.com/skills.

Cera. https://ceracare.co.uk/.

clarifai. https://www.clarifai.com/.

Connecterra. https://www.connecterra.io/.

Conversica. https://www.conversica.com/.

Corti—A co-pilot for medical interviews. https://corti.ai/.

Coursera. https://www.coursera.org/.

DarkTrace. https://www.darktrace.com/en/.

Darwin Ecosystem. https://www.darwinecosystem.com/.

Deloitte. https://www2.deloitte.com.

Dexter. https://docs.rundexter.com/.

Eyesight Technologies. https://www.eyesight-tech.com/.

Facebook—Artificial Intelligence. https://ai.facebook.com/tools/.

Gaggle. https://www.gaggle.net/.
GitHub. https://github.com/.
Google AI. https://ai.google/.
Google Cloud—AI & Machine Learning Products. https://cloud.google.com/products/ai/.
Graphcore. https://www.graphcore.ai/.
Hire Vue. https://www.hirevue.com/.
Honeywell—Intelligrated. https://www.intelligrated.com/en.
Human Brain Project. https://www.humanbrainproject.eu/en/.
IBM Research AI. https://www.research.ibm.com/artificial-intelligence/.
IBM—What's Next for AI? https://www.ibm.com/watson/advantage-reports/future-of-artificial-intelligence.html.
IDx. https://www.eyediagnosis.net/.
Kittyhawk. https://kittyhawk.io/.
Long Now Foundation. http://longnow.org/.
Microsoft—AI Business School. https://www.microsoft.com/en-us/ai/ai-business-school.
Microsoft—Azure Machine Learning Studio. https://azure.microsoft.com/en-us/services/machine-learning-studio/.
MindBridge. https://www.mindbridge.ai/.
Mobileye—an Intel company. https://www.mobileye.com/us/fleets/.
NASA.gov—Unmanned Aircraft. https://www.nasa.gov/subject/9566/unmanned-aircraft/.
Netflix Prize Forum. https://www.netflixprize.com/community/topic_1537.html.
Norman: World's First Psychopath AI. http://norman-ai.mit.edu/.
OpenAI. https://openai.com/.
Orcam. https://www.orcam.com/en/.
Overbond. https://www.overbond.com/.
People.ai. https://people.ai/.
Pryon—Augmented Intelligence in Action. https://www.pryon.com/.
Pymetrics. https://www.pymetrics.com/employers/.
Qualtrics. https://www.qualtrics.com/.
Qure. ai. http://qure.ai/.
Radiant Solutions. https://www.radiantsolutions.com/.
Rasa. https://rasa.com/.
Salesforce— Einstein. https://www.salesforce.com/products/einstein/overview/.
Sana Labs. http://sanalabs.com/.
securly:// https://www.securly.com/.
SenticNet: Helping machines to learn, leverage, love. https://sentic.net/.
Shield AI. https://www.shield.ai/.
Sigma Ai. https://www.sigma-ai.com/.
SiteXPro. https://www.sitexpro.com/.
Starkey Hearing Technologies. https://www.starkey.com/.
Stripe. https://stripe.com/.
Tact.ai. https://tact.ai/.
Taranis. http://www.taranis.ag/.
Telefónica, Aura.
https://aura.telefonica.com.
TextRecruit. https://www.textrecruit.com/.
Topbots. https://www.topbots.com/.
Transnorm. https://www.transnorm.com/en/home.html.
tusimple. https://www.tusimple.com/.

Ultimate   Software.   https://www.ultimatesoftware.com/UltiPro-Solution-Features-Xander-Perception.

Uptake—Industrial AI. https://www.uptake.com/.

Verily Life Sciences. https://verily.com/.

Wikipedia, public domain image. https://en.wikipedia.org/wiki/Regression_analysis.

World Intellectual Property Organization, Technology Trends 2019: Artificial Intelligence. https://www.wipo.int/edocs/pubdocs/en/wipo_pub_1055.pdf. The executive summary can be downloaded from https://www.wipo.int/edocs/pubdocs/en/wipo_pub_1055-exe_summary1.pdf.

Zipline. https://flyzipline.com/.

INDEX

Accenture, 51
Adobe, 65, 69
advanced driver assistance systems (ADAS), 85
Aerofarms, 91
Affectiva, 92
Affirm, 77
Alibaba, 61
AllyO, 81
Alphabet, 54, 63, 64, 71; Waymo, 85
Amazon, 44, 56, 61, 63, 64, 69, 85, 93, 164; Alexa, 18, 107; biased hiring algorithm, 89; Web Services, 34, 56–57
Amodo, 78
Apple, 60
Applied AI, 51
artificial intelligence (AI): adoption options, 51; algorithms, 33; assistance for the blind, 22, 58; bonanza, 43–44; brainless, 2, 3; cloud companies, 52–60; consistency, 42; content generation, 48–49; cost structure, 126–127, 137, 137–138; data importance, 19, 131; data processing, 17; data reliance, 5; delusions, 1; dependency, 42; design without

controls, 120; deep fakes, 49–50; doomsday scenario, 114–115; ethics. See ethics; foreign government support, 44, 74; firms' recognized need for, 45; fraud, 45; functions, 47–49; game performance, 12; governance, cybernetics, kubernetes, 123–125; government support, 44, 96; hardware, 60–62; implementation approaches, 51, 105–106; implementation control, 110–112; implementation leadership, 108–109; implementation organization, 104–107; implementation planning, 101–104; implementation resistance, 108–109, 109; in agriculture, 89–91; in customer support, 67–69; in education, 87–89; in finance and insurance, 75–79; in human resources (HR), 79–82; in marketing, advertising, and sales, 63–67; in medical industry, 70–74; in military, 95–97; in supply chain management and transportation, 83–87; in surveillance and security, 91–95; hubris, 117; hype bubble, 1;

ABOUT THE AUTHORS

Brennan Pursell, MBA, PhD, is professor of business and history at DeSales University and founder and director of its Applied AI Program. He teaches a wide range of courses in the undergraduate and MBA programs, and provides business consulting services to businesses large and small. *Outsmarting AI* is his fifth book. He lives with his family in the greater New York metropolitan area.

Joshua Walker, considered a pioneer in the emerging field of law and computer science, is the co-founder of both CodeX (Stanford Center for Legal Informatics) and Lex Machina—one of the first practical legal AI companies, regularly used by many of the Fortune 500, law firms, and all three branches of the US government. He is also the author of "On Legal AI" and is seeking to help architect the next generation of AI tools for regular folks. He and his family are based in San Francisco, California.